All Across China

Beijing

Tibet

Yunnan

Ellen Weisberg
&
Ken Yoffe

Published by:
Chipmunkapublishing
P.O Box 6872
Brentwood
Essex
CM13 1ZT
United Kingdom

http://www.chipmunkapublishing.com

Asia

Russia

Turkey
Israel Syria
Iraq
Jordan
Saudi Arabia
Yemen Oman
Iran
Afghanistan
Pakistan
Kazakhstan
Nepal
India
Mongolia
China
Myanmar
Thailand
Cambodia
Laos Vietnam
Korea
Japan
Taiwan
Philippines
Malaysia
Singapore
Indonesia
Sri Lanka

Welcome to China! China is the fourth largest country in the world, and has the world's largest population. Over a billion people, with different cultures and languages, live here! China is located in East Asia, and is full of breath-taking mountains and rivers, and many different animals.

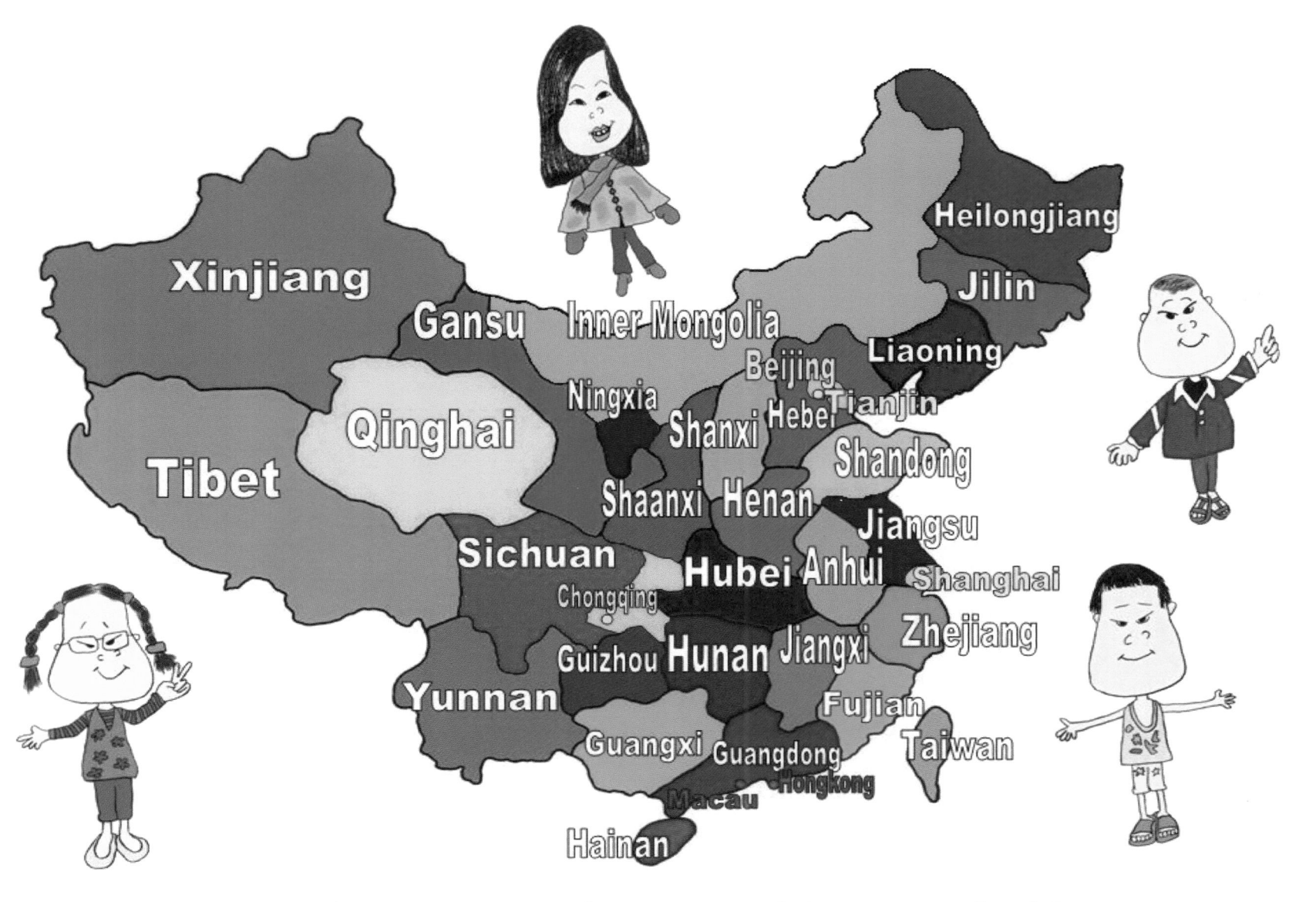

Four fun-loving friends, Ning, Cai, Na, and Song, are inviting you to journey with them through China's thirty-four provinces, municipalities, and other regions. At each stop, they'll introduce you to another friend who is named after the area's capital.

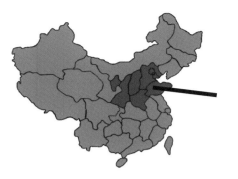

Ning

Four friends take a trip all around
and cover a large amount of ground.
Ning heads north to China's Great Wall.
Cai sees temples with statues so tall.
Na goes out where the water freezes,
while Song moves south to warm, warm breezes.
The capital city of each place they go
is also the name of a friend they know!

Cai

Na

Song

Cai in Central China

Shanghai

Anhui

Sichuan

Jiangsu

Yunnan

In central China, Cai follows the vast and lovely Yangtze, or "Long River." She hikes east through Yunnan and Sichuan before boarding a cruise ship in Chongqing. She then travels through the Yangtze Plain, passing her favorite lake, Dongting. Finally, she ends her trip in Shanghai, near the mouth of the Yangtze River.

Cai

Down the Yangtze River,
Cai makes her way
from the Sichuan Basin
to Chongqing and Hubei.
After passing through
Hunan and Jiangxi,
Cai goes to Shanghai
at the East China Sea.

Yangtze River   Yellow Sea

East China Sea

Central China   South China Sea

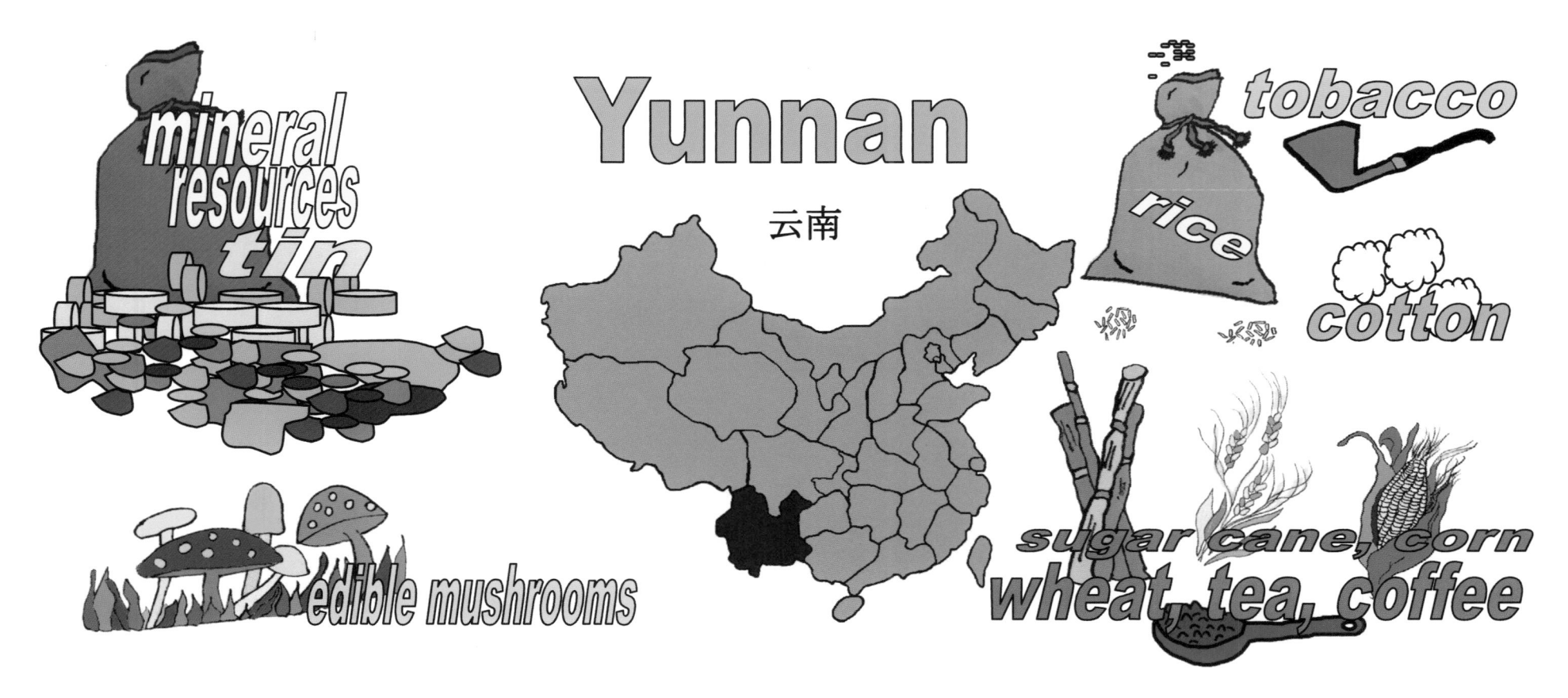

mineral resources
tin

edible mushrooms

Yunnan

云南

tobacco

rice

cotton

sugar cane, corn
wheat, tea, coffee

Cai's first visit is to her friend Kunming, who lives in Yunnan, home to the largest number of ethnic groups in China. The girls make their way over the vast mountain ranges and rivers in the northern part of the province, and continue to walk the very rugged terrain that extends into the western part of Yunnan. Kunming tells Cai that parts of Yunnan are tropical, and parts of it have snow-covered mountains. She proudly declares that Yunnan is home to around half of China's birds and mammals. They first visit Shangri-La County, a Tibetan township in the northwestern mountains. They then see the amazing Stone Forest, and finally Fuxian Lake, which is the second deepest lake in all of China.

Kunming passes by a tree.
A snub-nosed monkey she can see.
She then goes up to Shangri-La
to see her Tibetan ma and pa.

Kunming

Yunnan

"South of the Clouds"

Shangri-La

Yangtze River

Kunming

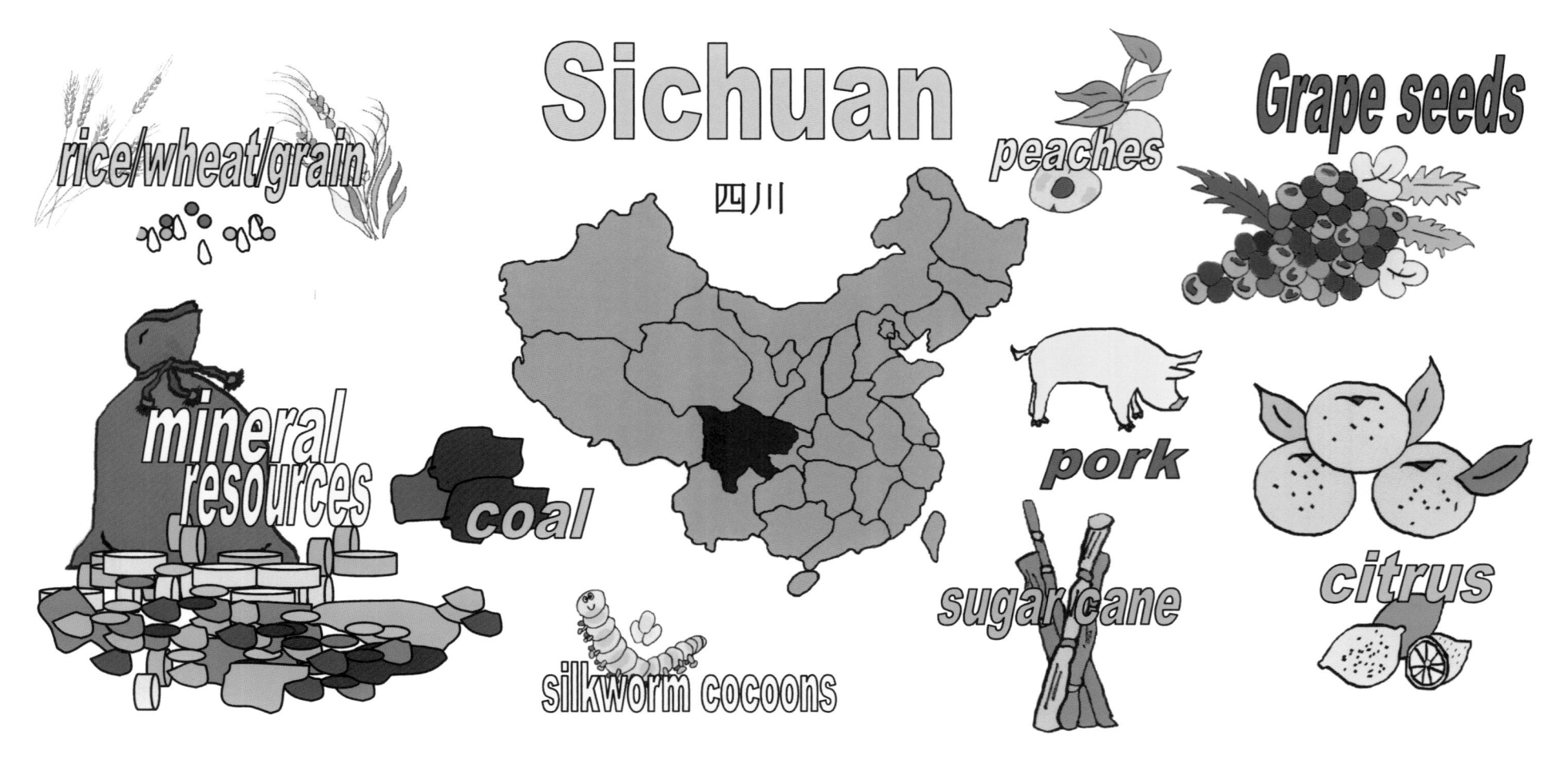

Cai's next journey is to see her friend, Chengdu, who lives in Sichuan province. Chengdu proudly explains to Cai that Sichuan is rich in mineral resources and a leader of agricultural production in China. She goes on to boast that Sichuan is one of China's most important industrial bases. Cai listens attentively while Chengdu talks, fascinated to learn that Sichuan was the most heavily populated province in China before Chongqing was separated from it. The girls continue their conversation over a spicy and hot Sichuan meal. Sichuan cuisine is extremely popular in China, and is, in fact, known all over the world.

Chengdu's food, filled with spice
is served to her in a bowl of rice.
With tongue on fire, she needs a drink
and runs fast toward the kitchen sink!

Sichuan

"Four Rivers"

Chengdu

Yangtze River

Yangtze River

Chengdu

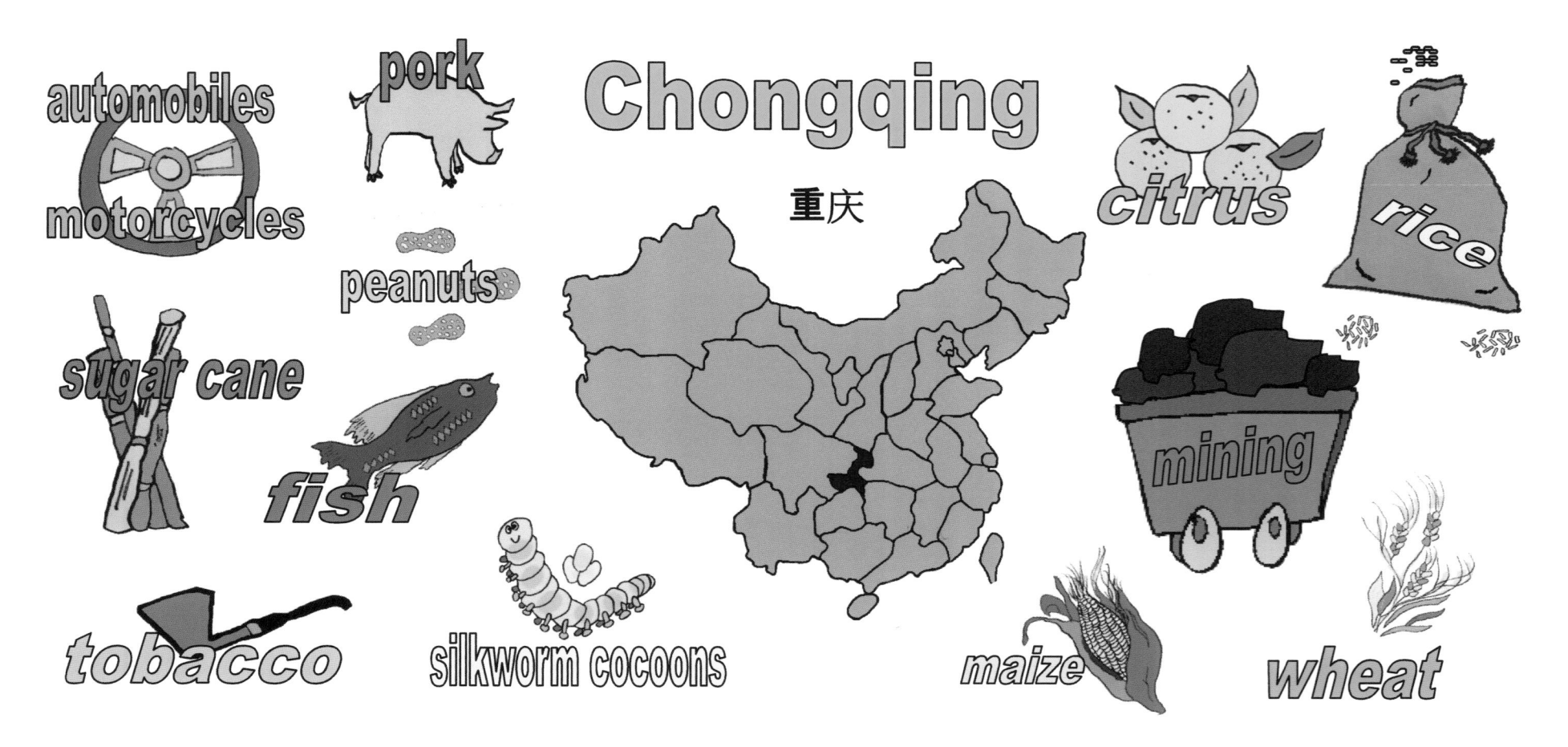

automobiles
motorcycles
pork
Chongqing
重庆
citrus
rice
peanuts
sugar cane
fish
mining
tobacco
silkworm cocoons
maize
wheat

Cai's next stop is the home of her lovely friend, Chongqing, who is named after the municipality where she lives. Chongqing's mother greets Cai with delicious hot pot, or Chinese fondue, a very spicy and popular dish. After they eat, Cai and Chongqing go into town to buy bamboo handcrafts and to visit the famous local zoo. They then get on a cruise boat to tour the Yangtze's Three Gorges, the Qutang (in Chongqing), the Wu (in Chongqing), and the Xiling (in Hubei). At nightfall, the girls take a pleasant stroll along the brightly lit, rolling hills that overlook the river.

Our pretty Chongqing
lives near the Yangtze.
Her skin is so soft,
her hair full and free.
She loves the pandas
she sees at the zoo,
and Sichuan pepper
in Chinese fondue.

Chongqing

Yangtze River

Chongqing

South China Sea

Chongqing

Wu Gorge

Yangtze River

Qutang Gorge

Chongqing City

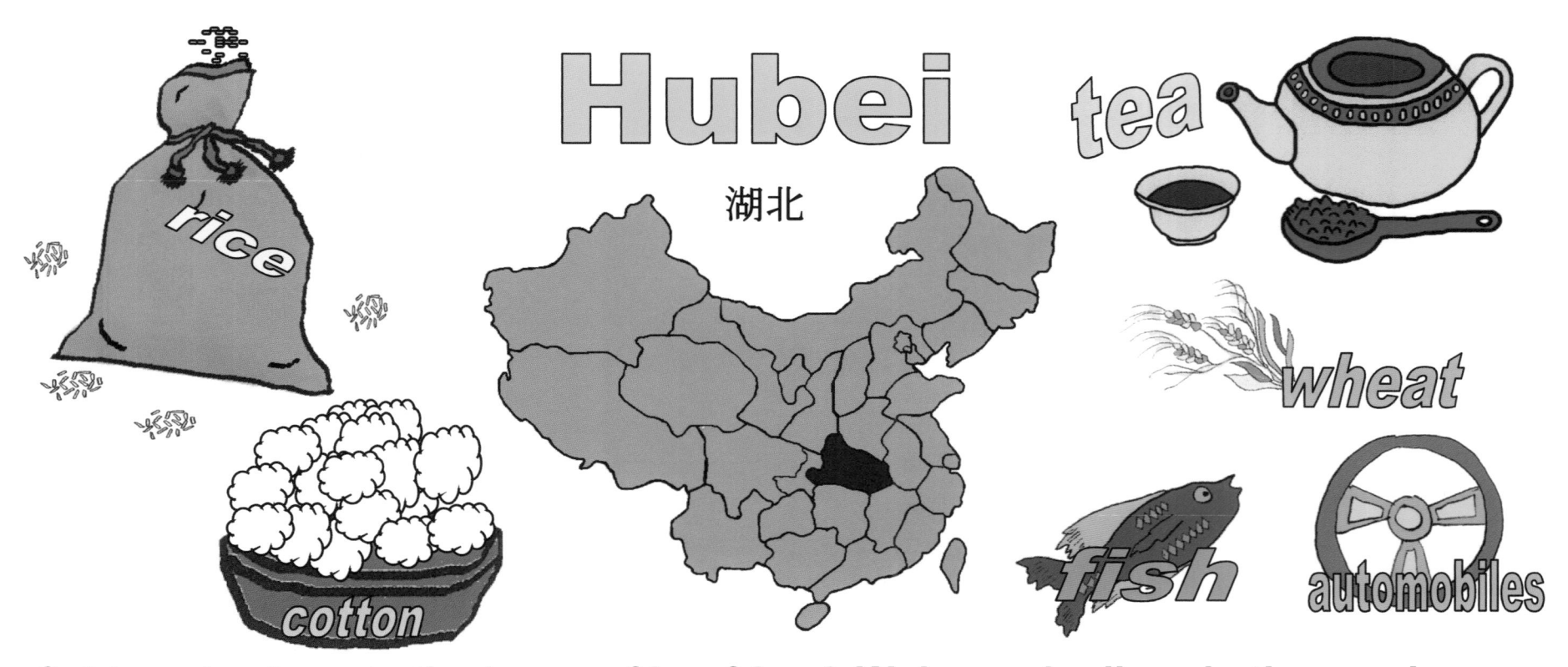

Hubei

湖北

rice

cotton

tea

wheat

fish

automobiles

Cai travels along to the home of her friend, Wuhan, who lives in the province of Hubei. Wuhan tells Cai that Hubei is located north of Dongting Lake, and is nicknamed "Province of Lakes" because of the thousands of lakes throughout the province. Hubei is also called the "Land of Fish and Rice." Cai and Wuhan sit down in a restaurant in the Three Gorges region, which is in the western part of the province where the Yangtze River enters. They hungrily eye a plate of Wuchang fish, which is a very popular dish in Hubei cuisine. Over their meal, Wuhan angrily tells Cai that Hubei residents are insultingly nicknamed "nine-headed birds," an aggressive and hard-to-kill mythological creature. He then more calmly explains that because of the tone and volume of his native dialect to outsiders, people from Hubei often sound like they're angry.

Wuhan goes from lake to stream
to find the biggest fish to steam.
He yells out loud when he hooks a winner.
Wuchang fish will be his dinner.

Wuhan

Hubei

"North of the Lake"

Wuhan

Yangtze River

Cai continues on her way to meet her friend Changsha, who lives in Hunan. Cai mentions to Changsha that she has just visited her friend Wuhan in Hubei, north of Lake Dongting. Changsha tells her that Hunan is mostly *south* of Lake Dongting, which is Hunan's largest lake. It is also China's second largest freshwater lake, while Poyang Lake in Jiangxi is China's largest. Cai and Changsha hike some of the mountains and hills of Hunan. The girls duck out of a downpour and into a restaurant where they enjoy a delicious traditional Hunan meal with lots of chili peppers. Their next visit is to the village of Shaoshan, the birthplace of Mao Zedong (also known as "The Great Helmsman"), the father of modern communist China, or the People's Republic of China. Their last, and favorite, stop is to a store where they buy some lovely craftwork.

Above the lake's
a rainy sky.
Changsha runs
to where it's dry.
In a shop,
she buys some jade,
and craftwork that
an artist made.

Hunan

"South of the Lake"

Changsha

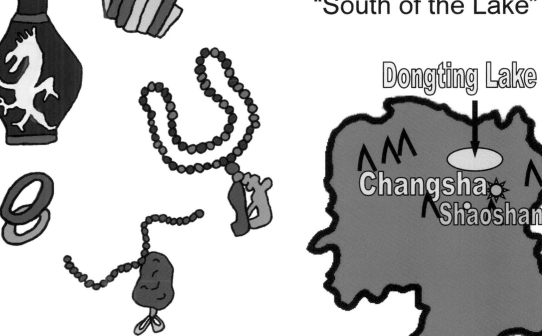

Dongting Lake

Changsha
Shaoshan

Jiangxi

江西

rice

porcelain

cotton

mineral resources

Cai moves onward to meet her good buddy, Nanchang, in northern Jiangxi. They first take a trip to the highest point in Jiangxi, Mount Huanggang in the Wuyi Mountains. They next go to Lake Poyang, which Nanchang proudly reminds Cai is the largest freshwater lake in China. At a nearby restaurant, they eat a plate of traditional Jiangxi cuisine. This strongly flavored cuisine makes heavy use of chili peppers, like that from Hunan. They then relax and watch a beautiful Jiangxi opera before visiting historic Longhushan, the birthplace of Taoism. Finally, they finish their day with some shopping. Cai picks up some lovely porcelain vases in one of the stores they visit in Jingdezhen. Nanchang boasts about how Jingdezhen is known as a producer of the best porcelain in China.

Jiangxi opera

Nanchang eats a peppery dish
and reddens in the face.
He cools off in big Lake Poyang,
then buys a porcelain vase.

Jiangxi
"West of the River"

Nanchang

Lake Poyang

Jingdezhen

Nanchang

Longhushan

Wuyi Mountains

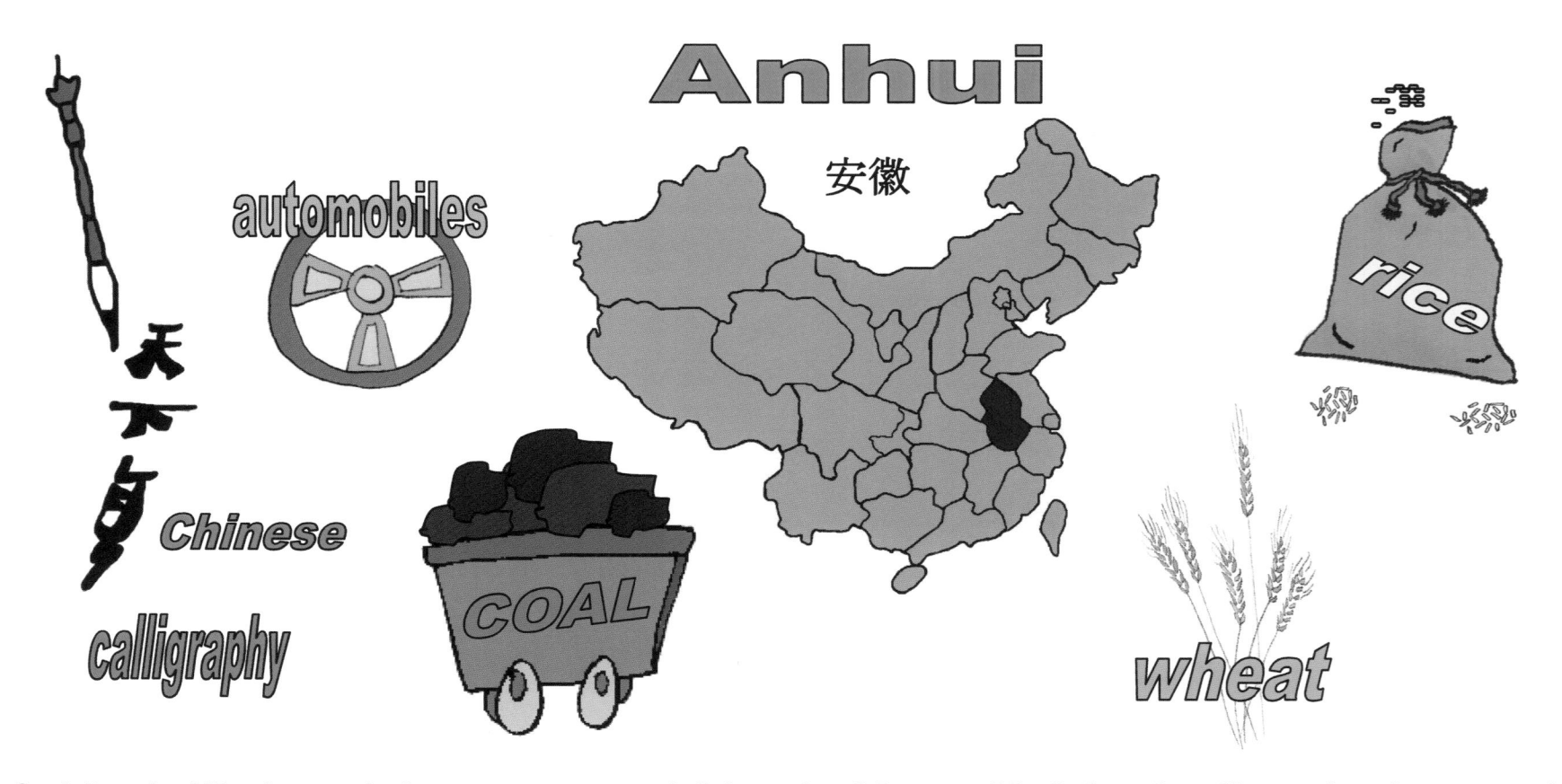

Cai is thrilled to visit a very good friend of hers, Hefei, who lives in the province of Anhui. Cai and Hefei first do some hiking in the Huangshan Mountains. They marvel at Lotus Peak, which is Anhui's highest point. They then visit an ancient village in southern Anhui, and enjoy a dinner of traditional Anhui cuisine, wild game with herbs. During her visit, Cai learns a lot about Chinese calligraphy. Hefei explains that Anhui is known for making many products related to the art, such as She inkstone, Xuan paper, and Hui ink.

Hefei goes down toward the south
for Anhui food and drink.
Then she walks in a little shop
to buy a stone for ink.

Jiangsu

江苏

cotton

peanuts

soybeans

fish

peaches

maize

rice

wheat

apples

silkworms

Cai is now off to visit Nanjing, who lives in the province of Jiangsu. They first go to southern Jiangsu, to the beautiful classical gardens in the city of Suzhou. Cai is amazed at the number of canals that have been built throughout the city. Nanjing explains to Cai that Suzhou is nicknamed "Venice of the East" because of all of its canals, and Jiangsu province has been nicknamed "Land of Water" because of its sophisticated irrigation system. Nanjing brags to Cai about Jiangsu being one of China's richest provinces, with southern Jiangsu famous for its prosperity. The girls visit Wuxi, where they see one of the world's tallest Buddha statues. Then they dine on traditional Jiangsu cuisine, which is very popular in China. They next visit the Sun Yat-sen Mausoleum. Sun Yat-sen overthrew the last Chinese emperor, and is known as the "Father of Chinese Democracy." Finally, they go to the Nanjing zoo, and enjoy a great show at the Nanjing circus.

Nanjing

Jiangsu

Yellow Sea

Nanjing

Wuxi

Suzhou

Nanjing walks right through Suzhou,
"the Venice of the East."
At Nanjing zoo, she sees giraffes
and other giant beasts.
In Wuxi there are temples huge,
and others that are small,
as well as Buddha statues that
are big and oh so tall.

Shanghai

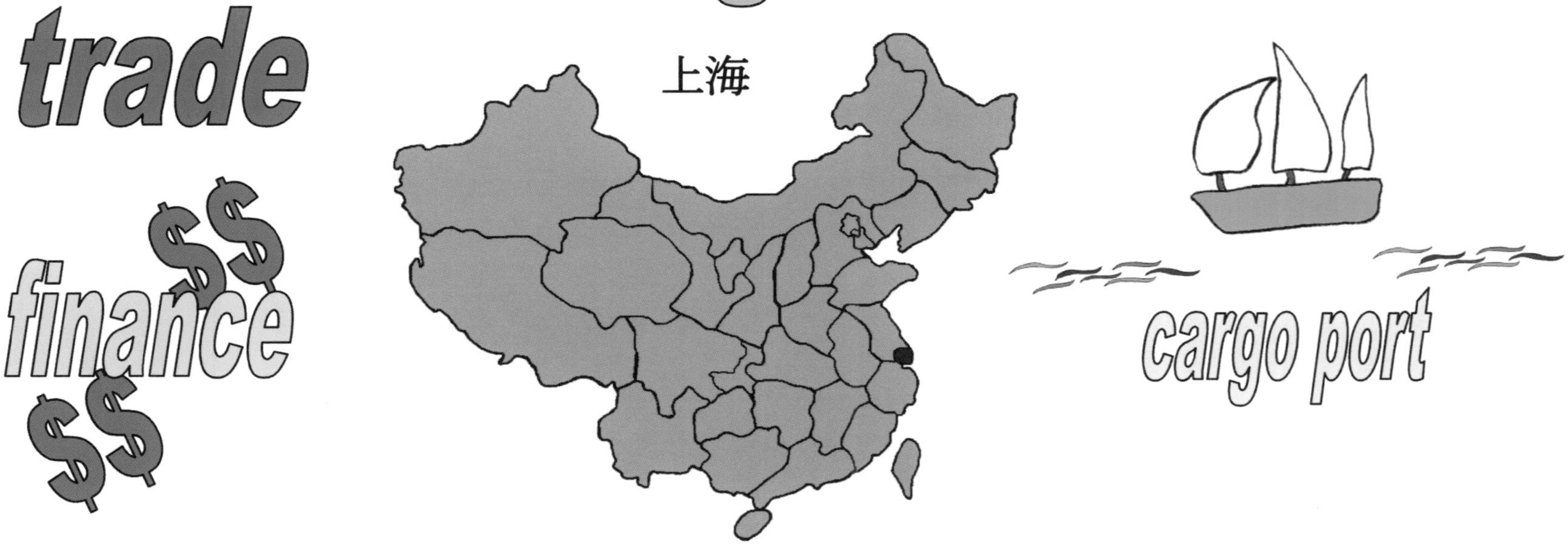

上海

trade

finance

$$ $$ $$

cargo port

Cai's final trip is to visit her pal, Shanghai, who was named after the municipality he lives in. It is one of China's four municipalities and is also China's largest city and center for trade and finance. Shanghai shows Cai why his home has been referred to as an example of the world's fastest-growing economy, with the world's busiest cargo port. Shanghai's Pudong District contains the Shanghai World Financial Center, which is the tallest skyscraper in China and the second tallest skyscraper in the world!

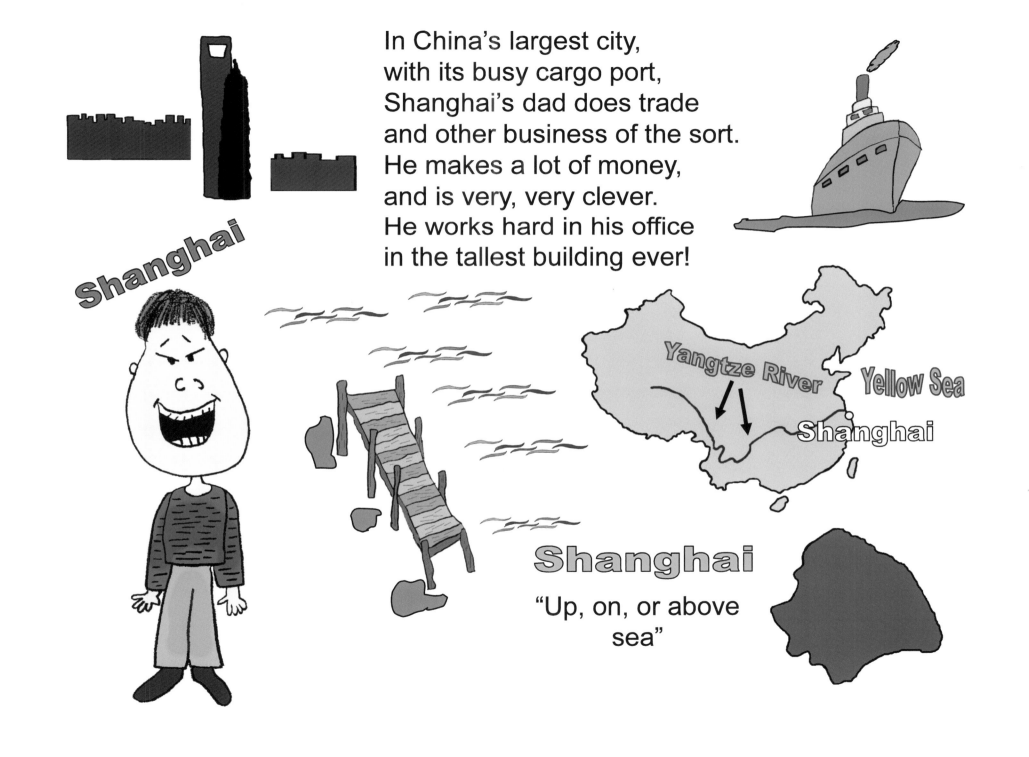

In China's largest city,
with its busy cargo port,
Shanghai's dad does trade
and other business of the sort.
He makes a lot of money,
and is very, very clever.
He works hard in his office
in the tallest building ever!

Shanghai

Yangtze River

Yellow Sea

Shanghai

Shanghai

"Up, on, or above sea"

Na in Northeast and Outer China

Heilongjiang
Jilin
Xinjiang
Liaoning
Tibet

Adventurous Na has quite a lot of traveling ahead of her! She has two major regions of China and many, many miles to cover. She begins in the incredibly high mountains of Tibet, and heads north and east to visit pals in Xinjiang, Qinghai, and the rest of Outer China. The second part of her journey is Northeast China, which includes cold Heilongjiang, Jilin and its opera, and the Ansham Buddha of Liaoning.

Na

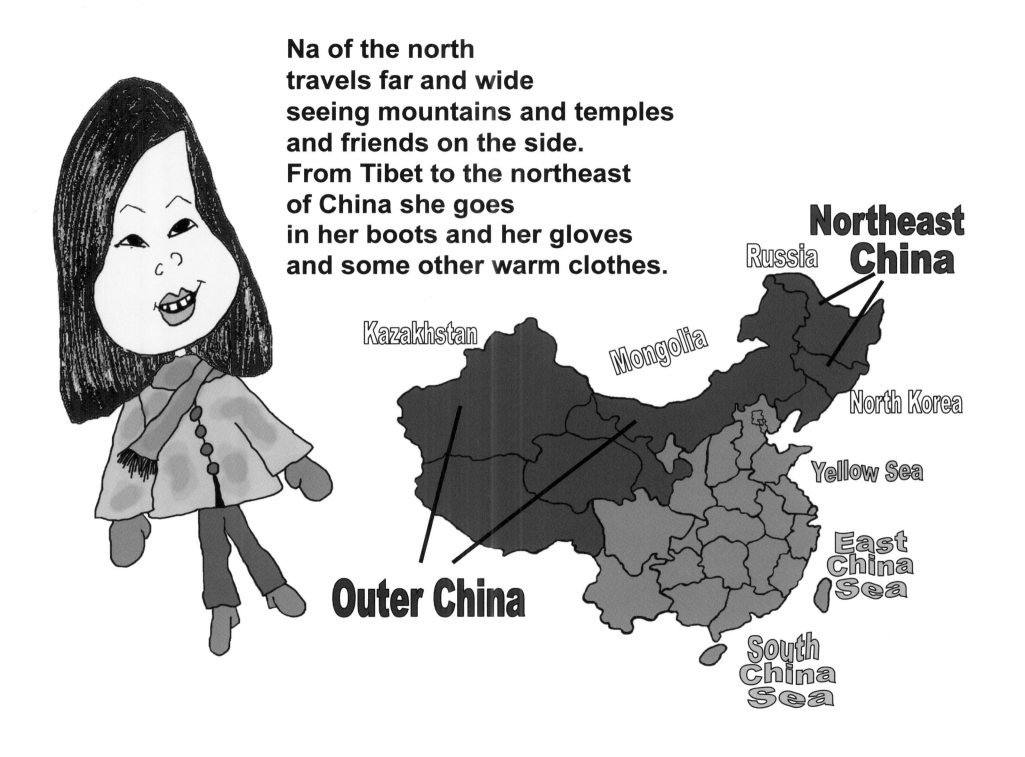

Na of the north
travels far and wide
seeing mountains and temples
and friends on the side.
From Tibet to the northeast
of China she goes
in her boots and her gloves
and some other warm clothes.

Tibet

wheat/barley

西藏

sheep

cattle

Na first sets out to meet up with her friend, Lhasa, who lives in the Special Autonomous Region of Tibet. Most of Tibet's inhabitants are ethnically Tibetan and practice Tibetan Buddhism. Na and Lhasa go sight-seeing, and visit the Tibetan Plateau and Himalaya Mountains, the highest region in the world! Na is excited to learn that on Tibet's border is Mount Everest, the highest mountain on the planet! Na learns that because of the mountains and other rough terrain, Tibet has the lowest population density in all of China.

Lhasa knows
where he wants to go…
Way up high
on the Tibetan Plateau.
Through many tall mountains
he makes his way…
Some temples he passes
where Buddhist monks pray.

sheep

oil

Xinjiang

新疆

wheat

silk

cotton

grapes

Na next travels to Xinjiang, a Special Autonomous Region in the People's Republic of China and the home of her friend, Urumqi. Urumqi is a member of the Uyghur, the largest ethnic group in Xinjiang. The Uyghur even outnumber the Han Chinese, which make up the vast majority of people in China. Na and Urumqi do some hiking in the Tien Shan Mountains, which separate the northern Dzungarian Basin from the Tarim Basin in the south. Suddenly, in the middle of their hike, they feel a little trembling of the earth below their feet! Na frighteningly looks at Urumqi, who calmly explains that Xinjiang is a major zone for earthquakes, and that what they're experiencing is a small quake. Urumqi tries to distract Na by telling her that within Xinjiang is the point of land that is furthest from any sea. This area is located in the Dzoosotoyn Elisen Desert.

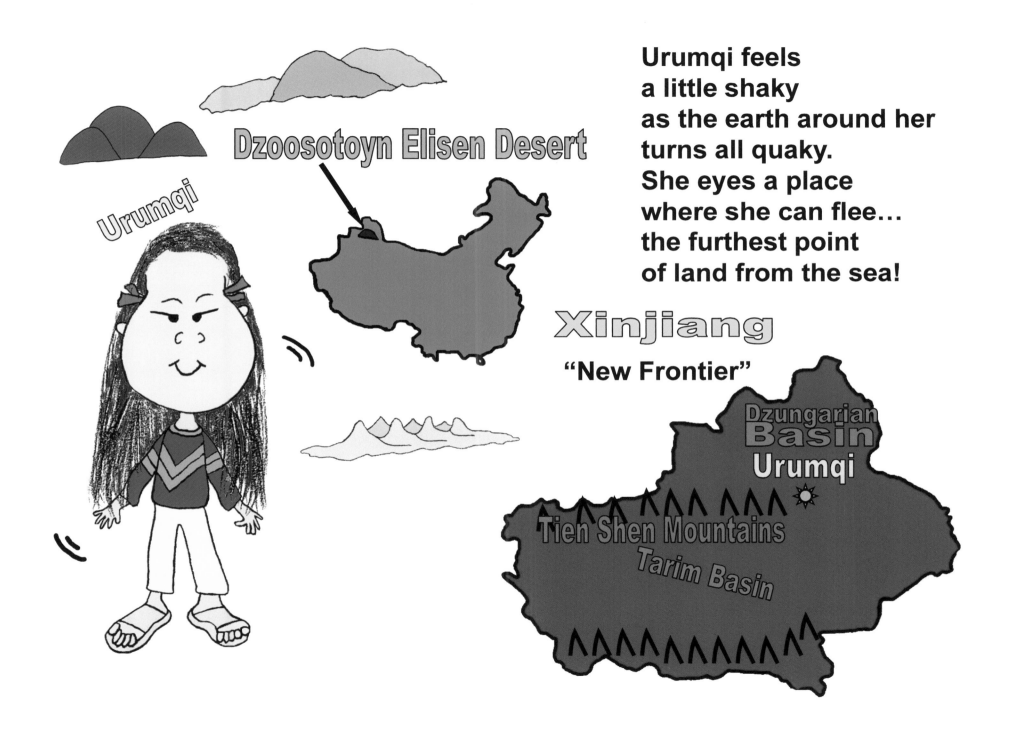

Urumqi feels
a little shaky
as the earth around her
turns all quaky.
She eyes a place
where she can flee…
the furthest point
of land from the sea!

sheep

Qinghai

青海

mining

wheat

oil

Na's next visit is with her friend, Xining, who lives in the province of Qinghai. Xining proudly declares to Na that Qinghai is the largest true province in all of China! Qinghai is named after beautiful Qinghai Lake, which is the largest saltwater lake in China. The girls travel to the Qinghai-Tibet plateau, also called the "Roof of the World," where the lake sits. They then take a ride on the Lanqing Railway, which is the major transportation route in and out of Qinghai. While the girls visit such wonderful attractions as the Great Mosque of Xining and the North Mountain Temple, they cling tightly to each other and shield their eyes from the sand blowing in their faces. Xining explains to Na that during the early months of the year, from February to April, Qinghai is affected by heavy winds and sandstorms.

There's lots of sand
in the air that blows.
Xining shields
her eyes and nose.
To temples and mosques,
some trips she'll take,
as well as a ride
to Qinghai lake.

Xining

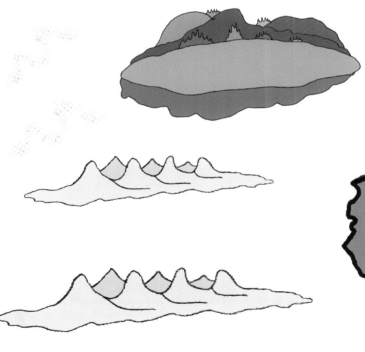

Qinghai
"Blue Sea"

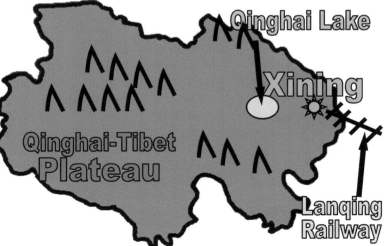

Qinghai Lake

Xining

Qinghai-Tibet
Plateau

Lanqing
Railway

Gansu

甘肃

oil

mining

cotton

wheat

maize

medicinal herbs

Na now travels to the home of her Han friend, Lanzhou, who lives in the province of Gansu, where the center of China is located. The two take a hike along a stretch in the Qilian Mountains, before heading off to see the most western pass of the Great Wall, Jiayuguan Pass. Na and Lanzhou have a quick meal of lamian, or pulled noodles, before exploring Silk Road, along which merchants used to travel. They also visit Mogao Grottoes near Dunhuang, which are cave temples filled with Buddhist art. The pair finally ride camels that take them to sand dunes on the edge of Dunhuang, where they have fun sledding down the sand slopes!

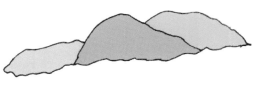

Lanzhou sees the greatest pass
of China's big Great Wall.
Then he glides down sand dunes
and has himself a ball.
He takes a lovely boat ride
in Gansu's southern part,
before exploring temples
that are filled with Buddhist art.

Lanzhou

Gansu

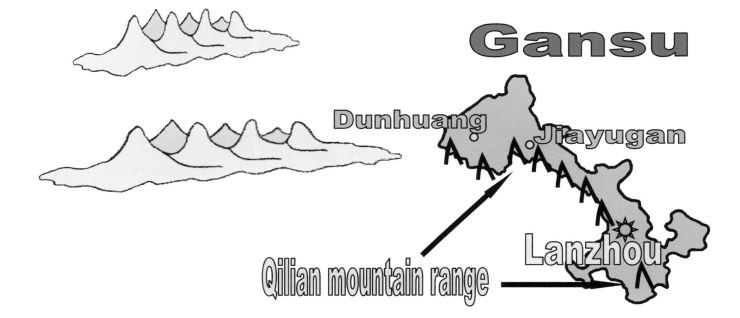

Dunhuang
Jiayugan
Lanzhou
Qilian mountain range

Inner Mongolia

内蒙古

coal

sheep & goats

wheat

winemaking

Na continues her journey to visit her friend, Hohhot, who lives in Inner Mongolia, which is the Mongol Special Autonomous Region of the People's Republic of China. Hohhot explains to Na that most of the people living in Inner Mongolia are Han Chinese, however Mongols are the second largest ethnic group there. Hohhot takes Na to see the Dazhao Temple, which has a silver statue of Buddha, murals, and dragon carvings. They also go to see the mausoleum of the Mongol founder, Genghis Khan. As a special treat, Hohhot brings Na to see a performance of circus acrobatics, which is popular in Inner Mongolia.

Hohhot

Hohhot is Chinese
and his ethnic group is Han.
In school he has some Mongol friends
and learns of Genghis Khan.
For a classroom field trip
to the circus Hohhot goes
to watch some acrobatics
and the very best of shows!

Inner Mongolia
(Nai Mongul)

Hohhot

Na now makes her way to Heilongjiang, which is the home of her friend, Harbin. Na is glad she didn't lose her scarf and mittens while visiting all of her other friends, because Heilongjiang is cold, cold, cold! She and Harbin start off the visit with hiking in the plentiful mountains and forests, which Harbin explains are home to animals like the Siberian Tiger, red-crowned crane, and lynx. And speaking of animals, Harbin goes on to tell Na that Heilongjiang has the largest number of milk cows in all of China, making it the biggest producer of milk in all of China's provinces. After hiking, the two friends enjoy watching a game of ice hockey before going to a very impressive ice sculpture exhibition.

Harbin stands in the cold, cold air,
wishing he had more clothes to wear.
But the winter freeze makes really great ice
to skate on and carve into shapes so nice!

Harbin

Heilongjiang
"Black Dragon River"

Harbin

Jilin

吉林

automobiles

maize

lumber

rice

The next stop for Na is the home of her fun-loving friend, Changchun, who is from a family of sheep-herders living in western Jilin province. The girls first start out hiking in the Changbai Mountains, where they pass Jilin's highest point, Baiyun Peak. While there, they see the gorgeous scenery at Heaven Lake. They then gaze at the famous "rime ice" on the branches of trees along the banks of the Songhua, which is the only river there that does not freeze in the winter. Na is amazed to learn that during the winter, people actually take a "winter swim," especially in nearby Jilin City. Just the thought of it makes Na shiver. Changchun takes Na to see a wonderful performance of Jilin opera, which is entertainment that is unique to the province. This is followed by a visit to a Karaoke club. Finally, they both visit Longtou Mountain to see its famous ancient tombs.

Changchun herds her sheep out west,
then plans to take a nice long rest.
To Heaven Lake she makes her way,
a lovely, scenic place to stay.

Jilin Opera

Jilin
"Lucky Forest"

Jilin City

Changbai Mountains

Changchun

Yalu River

Baiyun Peak
(and Heaven Lake)

Changchun

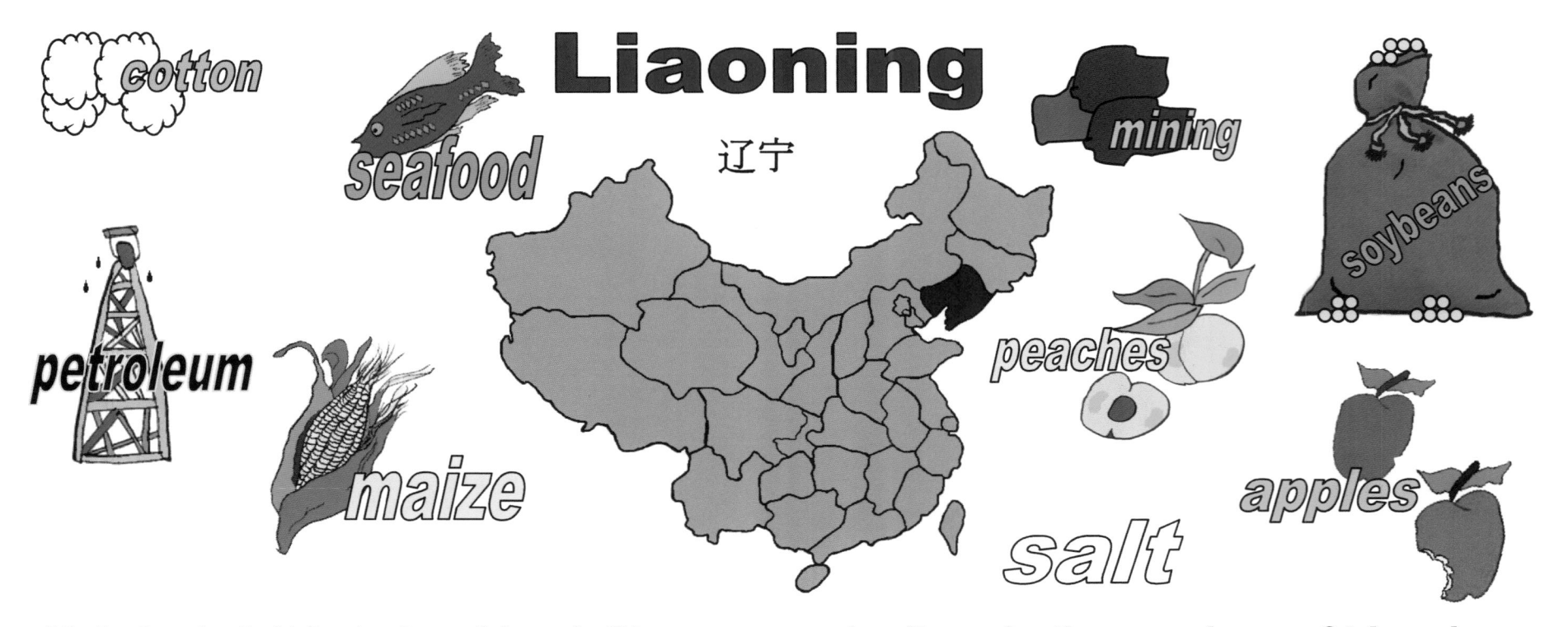

Liaoning

辽宁

cotton

seafood

mining

soybeans

petroleum

peaches

maize

salt

apples

Na's last visit is to her friend, Shenyang, who lives in the province of Liaoning. Like Jilin, Liaoning borders North Korea, with the Yalu River separating the two provinces from North Korea. Na and Shenyang do a lot of traveling across Liaoning, starting in the western highlands, where the Nulu'erhu Mountains sit, then easing their way across the central plains, and finally ending their travels in the hills of eastern Liaoning. Here, they visit Liaoning's highest point, Mount Huabozi, located in the Liaodong Peninsula. During their journey, Na and Shenyang visit the Mukden Palace, which belonged to the Qing Dynasty emperors. They also visit Anshan, where the Anshan Jade Buddha statue is, the largest in the entire world! Finally, they go to the port city of Dalian, which has shopping, beaches, and streetcars.

Shenyang

Shenyang hikes through mountains
that are covering the west.
He travels eastward toward the hills
before he takes a rest.
He thinks about how wonderful
the trip was that he made.
He even got to see a
Buddha statue made of jade.

Ning in Northern China

Ning gets ready for quite a long journey. He starts to follow along the Yellow River in Ningxia. Then he takes a plane to the border of Shaanxi and Shanxi, and he continues along the river through Henan and Shandong. His last visit is to Hebei, and the wonderful municipalities of Tianjin and Beijing, where he visits the famous Great Wall.

Ning

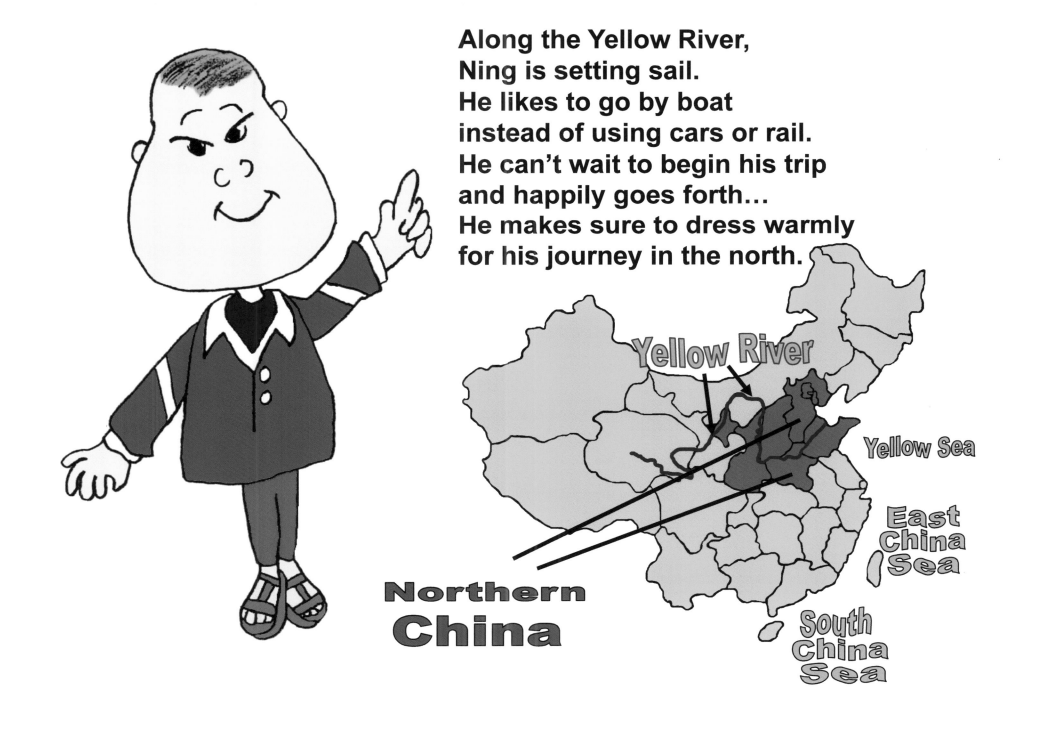

Along the Yellow River,
Ning is setting sail.
He likes to go by boat
instead of using cars or rail.
He can't wait to begin his trip
and happily goes forth…
He makes sure to dress warmly
for his journey in the north.

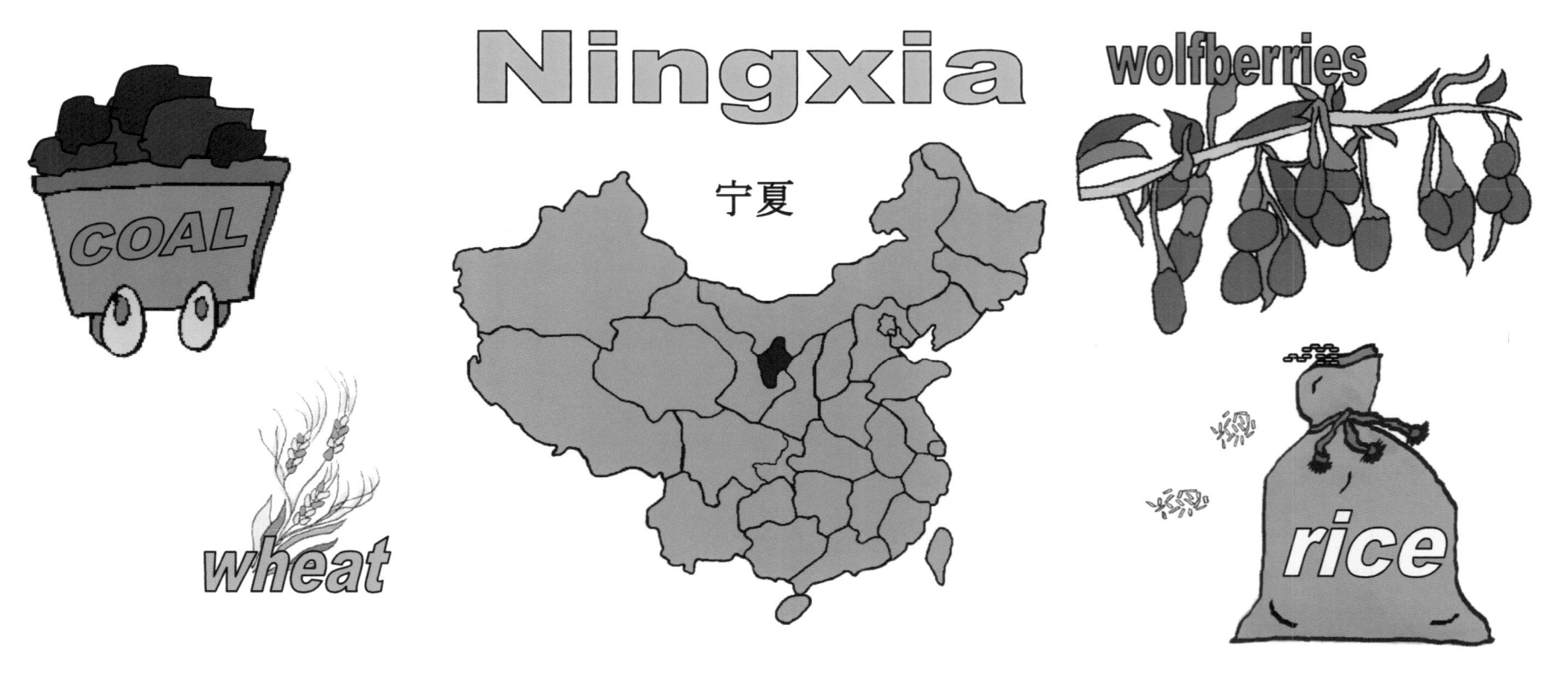

Ning's very first visit is with his friend, Yinchuan, a Hui who lives in the dry and desert-like autonomous region, Ningxia. The two eat lunch, and munch on wolfberries, which is a commonly eaten fruit in Ningxia (the main region in China where wolfberries are grown). The two friends visit Sand Lake Scenic Resort, where they have a lot of fun sliding down sand dunes, and going fishing and bird watching. They then visit the famous West Xia Imperial Tombs in ancient Yinchuan City, which is 1,000 years old! Ningxia is known as the "Great Wall Museum" because it contains ruins of the Ming and Qing walls. They finish Ning's visit with a trip to the very lovely and scenic Lipupan Mountain.

Yinchuan

Ningxia

Sand Lake

Yinchuan

Lipupan
Mountain

Yinchuan eats some wolfberries,
not far from where they're grown.
He then goes to Sand Lake to do
some fishing on his own.
After that the sand dunes will
await him for some sliding.
Then he'll look for birds to see
in what trees they are hiding.

Shaanxi

陕西

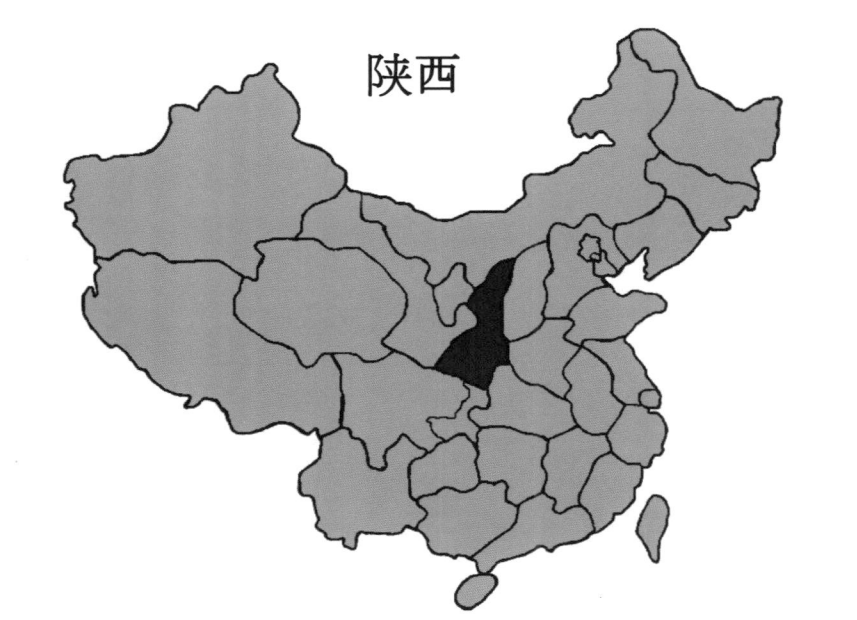

Ning's next destination is Shaanxi, where his friend Xi'an lives. The two first enjoy Qinqiang, or folk opera, which is a popular form of entertainment in Shaanxi. They then go to visit Mount Hua, one of the most famous mountains in China, and this is followed by a visit to the Mausoleum and Terracotta Army Museum of the First Qing Emperor in Xi'an. In fact, the city Xi'an is over 3,000 years old and is considered one of the most famous ancient cities in the world. They finish their day with dinner at a restaurant where they eat a dish consisting of Biang Biang noodles, which is referred to as one of the "ten strange wonders of Shaanxi." The noodles are so thick and long that they are described as being like a belt.

Xi'an

Qinqiang

Xi'an is so smart and
his intelligence is oodles.
He thinks about all sorts of things
while eating Biang Biang noodles.
The Terracotta Army,
all the temples and museums,
are what go through his mind
as well as Shaanxi's mausoleums.

Shaanxi

Yellow River

Xi'an

Mt. Hua

Shanxi

山西

Ning keeps traveling and visits his pal, Taiyuan, who lives in the sunny and dry province of Shanxi. The two boys visit the Great Wall of China, which makes up most of the northern border between Shanxi and Inner Mongolia. They next go for a boat ride along the Yellow River, which makes up the western border of Shanxi. While traveling the river, they see Hukou Waterfall, which is the second largest waterfall in China. They make a quick visit to Taiyuan's home, where Ning meets Taiyuan's father, who is a coal miner. Taiyuan explains to Ning that Shangxi is a leading producer of China's coal supplies. They then finish up their day listening to a performance of Shanxi opera, followed by a jaunt to Mount Wutai, the highest point in Shanxi and a Buddhist pilgrimage destination.

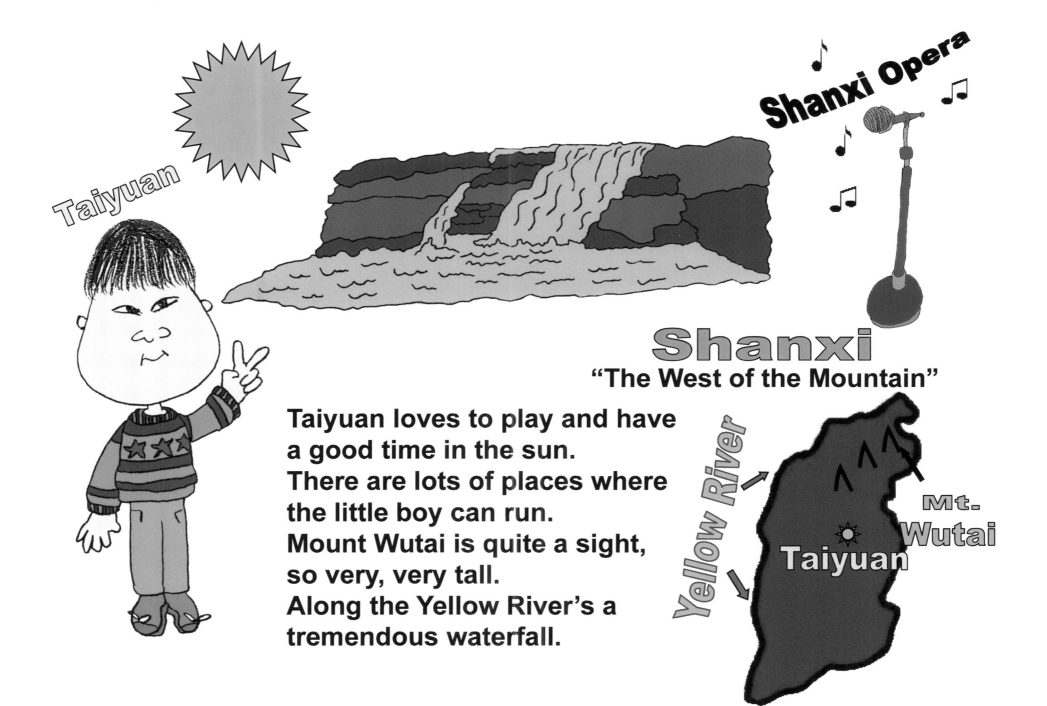

Taiyuan loves to play and have
a good time in the sun.
There are lots of places where
the little boy can run.
Mount Wutai is quite a sight,
so very, very tall.
Along the Yellow River's a
tremendous waterfall.

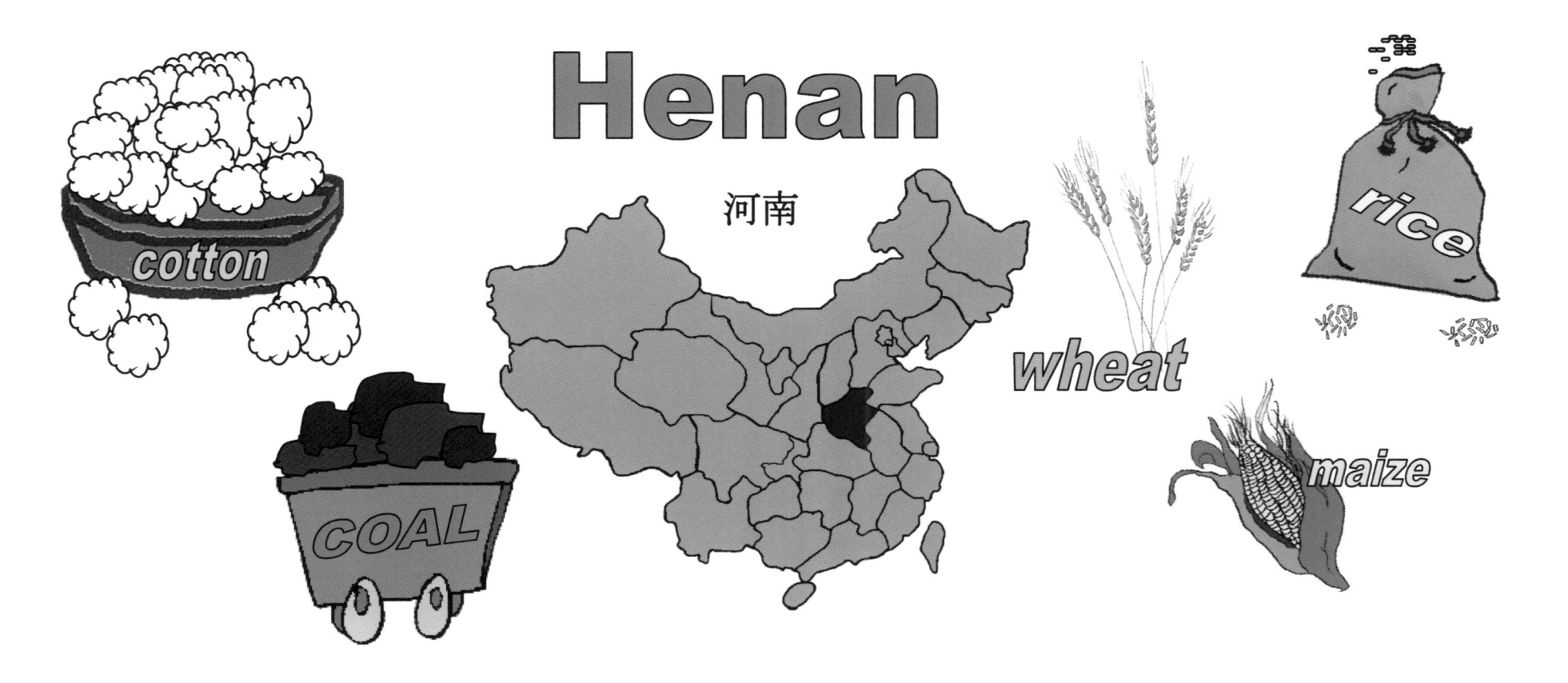

Henan

河南

cotton

COAL

wheat

rice

maize

Ning's next visit is to the home of his Han friend, Zhengzhou, who lives in Henan province. Ning tells Zhengzhou about all the people he saw while visiting Taiyuan in Shanxi. Zhengzhou laughs and tells Ning that he hasn't seen anything yet! She explains that Henan is the most populated province in all of China. The two pals do some sight-seeing in the Yellow River Valley. Ancient people lived in this region, and so it has among China's most historic relics. Zhengzhou informs Ning that the Yellow River runs through northern Henan.

In the Yellow River Valley, Zhengzhou spends her day… pushing through the people that are standing in her way.
To see through all the crowds she really has to strain.
She hopes fewer people live in the North China Plain.

Zhengzhou

Henan

"South of the (Yellow) River"

Yellow River

Zhengzhou

North China Plain

Shandong

山东

Ning moves along to visit his friend, Jinan, who lives in Shandong province east of Hebei. Jinan boasts to Ning that Shandong is one of the economically richer provinces in China, leading in industry and manufacturing. Jinan has relatives that live on the Shandong Peninsula, which is the richest part of the province. They pass many people in their travels, and Jinan tells Ning that Shandong is the second most heavily populated province in all of China, next to Henan. The friends decide to eat some lunch, and they stop in at a restaurant serving traditional Shandong cuisine, which is very popular in China. After they eat, they continue traveling by car along one of the longest expressways in China. They visit the very famous Temple and Cemetery of Confucius before calling it a day.

Shandong is the place
where little Jinan lives.
He loves it for the comfort
and the riches that it gives.
The Chinese sage Confucius
made his home there in B.C.
Confucius say Shandong
is just an awesome place to be!

Jinan

Shandong
"East of the Mountain"

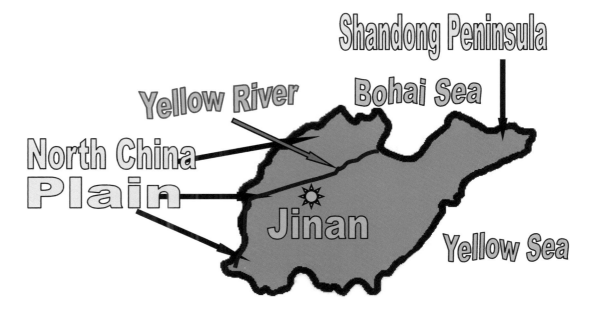

Shandong Peninsula

Bohai Sea

Yellow River

North China
Plain

Jinan

Yellow Sea

Hebei

河北

cotton

petroleum

maize

peanuts

wheat

COAL

Ning continues his journey and meets his friend, Shijiazhuang, or "Shi," who lives in the province of Hebei. The two friends first visit the Ming Great Wall in northern Hebei. They then ride a Jingguang Railway train and pass through several of Hebei's cities, admiring the beautiful pagodas and palaces. Along the way, they stop into a little store in Quyang County to browse of its famed Dingzhou porcelain. Their final visit is to the Zhaozhou Anji Bridge, which is China's oldest stone arch bridge.

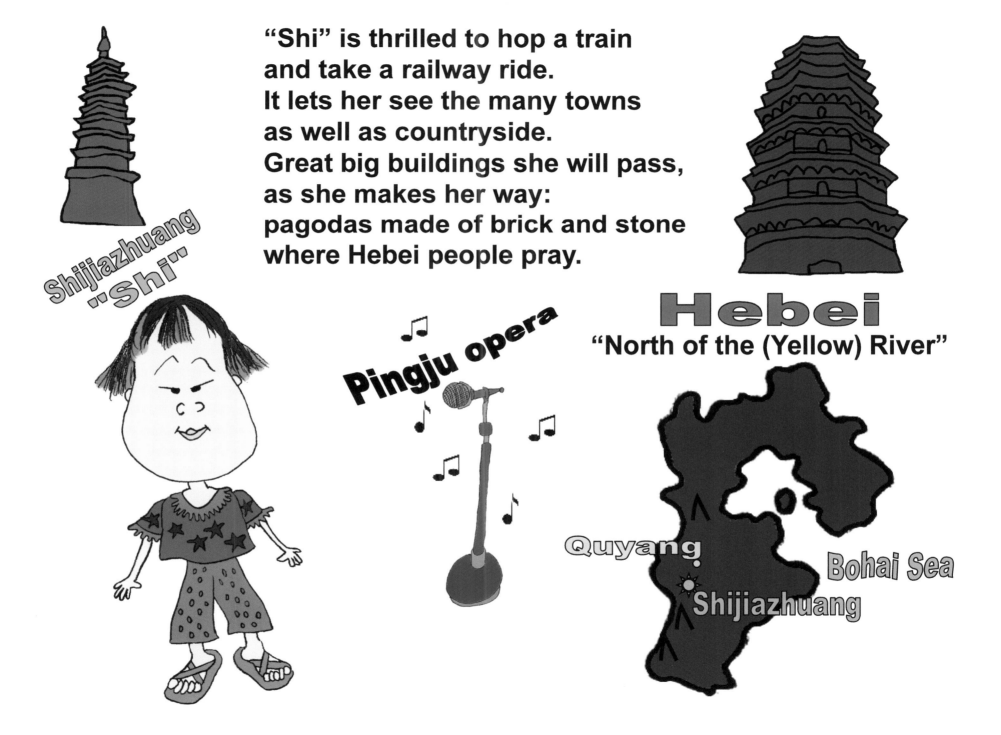

"Shi" is thrilled to hop a train
and take a railway ride.
It lets her see the many towns
as well as countryside.
Great big buildings she will pass,
as she makes her way:
pagodas made of brick and stone
where Hebei people pray.

Shijiazhuang "Shi"

Pingju opera

Hebei
"North of the (Yellow) River"

Quyang

Shijiazhuang

Bohai Sea

Ning travels a short distance to visit another friend, Tianjin, who is named after the municipality in which he lives. Tianjin is one of the four municipalities in China, its city being the third largest in China next to Shanghai and Beijing. The two friends sit down to a delightful meal of Tianjin cuisine, which Ning notices has a lot of fish in it. Ning dines on a dish called the "Eight Great Bowls," while Tianjin eats a dish called the "Four Great Stews." As Ning sprinkles some salt on his food, Tianjin informs him that his home is a great producer of salt in China. The two friends overhear someone in the restaurant say "the Tianjin mouth." Ning's friend explains to him that it is a commonly used phrase that refers to the nature of the Tianjin people, which is considered humorous. Both boys finish up their day by taking a stroll around Drum Tower Street, where they admire buildings reminiscent of the Qing Dynasty.

The Four Great Stews
were eaten in one sitting.
Tianjin now worries that
his clothes will all stop fitting.
He gets his body moving.
To Drum Tower Street he strolls.
At a local restaurant
he eats the Eight Great Bowls.

Tianjin

Tianjin
Yangtze River
Yellow Sea
East China Sea
South China Sea

Tianjin
"The Heavenly Ford"

Beijing

北京

wheat

maize

Ning is extremely excited about his last visit to his friend, Beijing, named after the municipality that he lives in. Beijing, the capital of China, is also the second largest city in the country (next to Shanghai), and is considered to be the cultural, political, and educational center of China. The two pals ride a train that is part of the largest railway system in China. They pass by some of Beijing's most beautiful palaces and temples. Later, they see the famous Great Wall of China, as well as the Forbidden City, the original residence of the emperors of the Ming and Qing dynasties. They also visit Tian'anmen (Gate of Heavenly Peace), Tian'anmen Square, and Zhongnanhai, which is the residence of the leaders of the People's Republic of China. After a very busy day of sight-seeing and traveling, the two friends dine on traditional Mandarin cuisine, such as the very popular Peking Roast Duck.

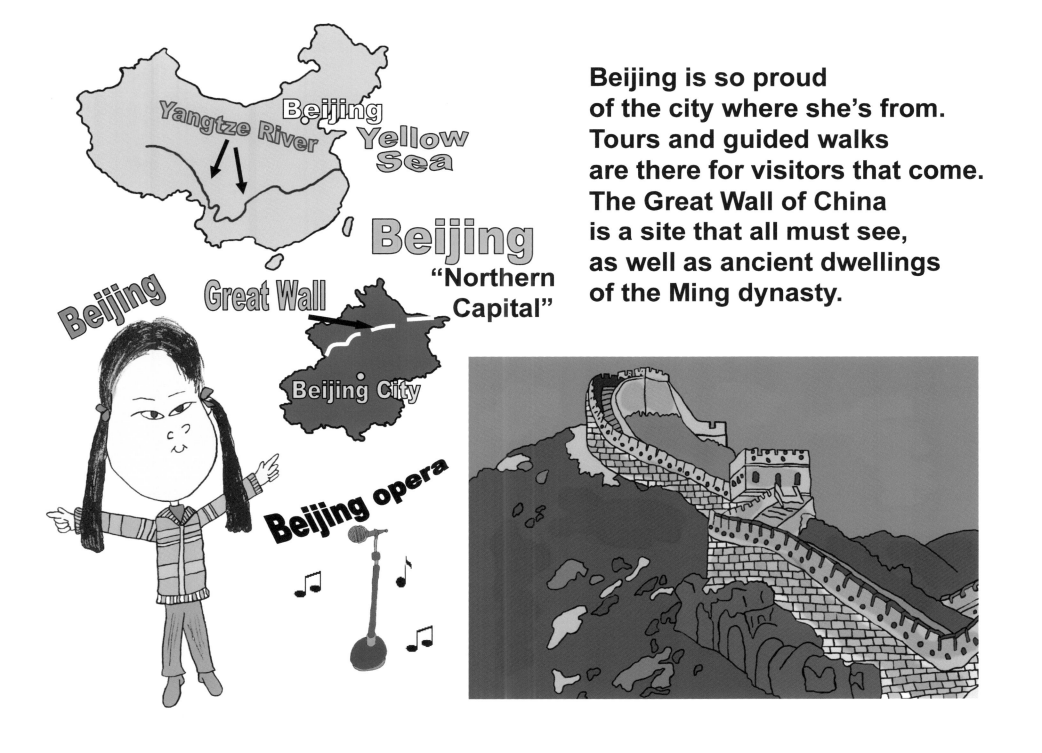

Beijing is so proud
of the city where she's from.
Tours and guided walks
are there for visitors that come.
The Great Wall of China
is a site that all must see,
as well as ancient dwellings
of the Ming dynasty.

Song in Southern China

Zhejiang

Fujian

Guizhou

Guangdong

Guangxi

Summery Song gets ready for a trip through some of China's most tropical and loveliest regions. He begins in the disputed area of Taiwan. Then he travels to Zhejiang, "The Land of Fish and Rice," and continues through Fujian and Guangdong to the Special Administrative Regions of Macau and Hong Kong. He suns himself on the gorgeous tropical beaches of Hainan, before experiencing the enlightening ethnic minority cultures of Guangxi and Guizhou.

Song

Song is in the southern part
of China near the sea.
The breezes, sun, and sand
make it a lovely place to be.
With fish and rice aplenty,
he has his share to eat…
and many different people
all around for him to meet.

Southern China

Yellow Sea

East
China
Sea

Vietnam

South
China
Sea

tea

sugar cane

Taiwan

台湾

rice

Song's first visit is to Taipei, a friend of his who lives in a disputed area. Her home of Taiwan is claimed by, but not controlled by, the People's Republic of China. Rather, it is controlled by the Republic of China (called "Taiwan"). Song and his friend ambitiously set out to visit all of Taiwan's islands, of which there are eighty-eight! They venture out, but suddenly find themselves in the midst of a downpour and seek shelter in a nearby restaurant. As they dine on some seafood, Song learns that rain is a common occurrence in the area, which is strongly affected by typhoons. The one nice thing about all of the rain that Taiwan gets is that forests stay green and flowers blossom all year round. During their meal, Song is also told that Taiwan is known as the "Kingdom of Coral," contributing to 80% of the world's coral production!

Taipei sees cloudy skies,
and many, many showers.
But with the rain comes plants and trees,
and lots of pretty flowers.
There's coral in the waters
and islands in the sea.
Taipei thinks her home is just
the greatest place to be!

Taiwan

East China Sea

Taipei

South China Sea

Zhejiang

浙江

fish

cotton

tea

wheat

rice

silkworm cocoons

Song next visits his good buddy, Hangzhou, who lives in the hilly province of Zhejiang. Hangzhou tells Song that the meaning of Zhejiang, "Crooked River," refers to the Qiantang River that flows through the province. The two boys first take a leisurely trip to one of the over 3,000 islands lining Zhejiang's coast. Upon arriving, they find a nice restaurant to go to and enjoy traditional Zhejiang cuisine, which is very popular in China. They also drink Longjing tea, one of the most prestigious teas in the country. While they eat, Hangzhou boasts to Song about northern Zhejiang being famed for its prosperity. He goes on to talk about his father, who is a rice farmer. He also mentions that Zhejiang is known as the "Land of Fish and Rice," with rice being its main crop, and the Zhoushan fishery being the largest fishery in the country. They do some shopping and find beautiful silk umbrellas and folding fans to purchase. Their last visit together is to the Baoguo Temple, the oldest intact wooden structure in southern China.

Hangzhou's dad's a farmer in the "Land of Fish and Rice." They grow a bunch of crops for Zhejiang dishes that are nice. Their hard work also lets them go on many shopping sprees, so they can buy umbrellas and silk fans and fancy teas.

Zhejiang

"Crooked River"

Hangzhou

Hangzhou Bay

Qiantang River

East China Sea

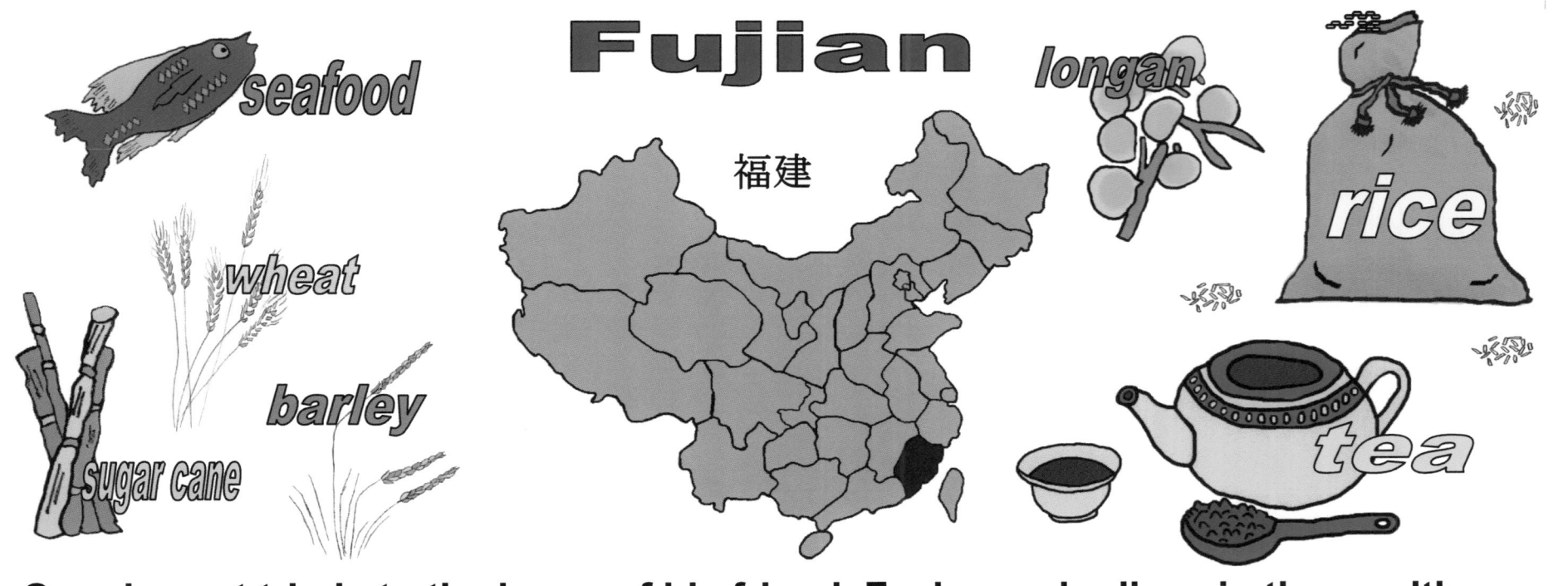

Fujian

福建

seafood

wheat

barley

sugar cane

longan

rice

tea

Song's next trip is to the home of his friend, Fuzhou, who lives in the wealthy province of Fujian. They do some hiking along the Wuyi Mountains, which make up part of the border between Fujian and the province of Jiangxi. There are, in fact, many mountains and cliffs throughout Fujian, although very little farmland, and the province has been described as "eight parts mountain, one part water, and one part farmland." Because of the way the mountains separate and isolate regions where people live, there are many different languages throughout Fujian. There is a saying, "If you drive five miles in Fujian the culture changes, and if you drive 10 miles, the language does." Song and Fuzhou watch some Fujian opera before dining on some traditional Fujian cuisine, which makes heavy use of seafood and is very popular in China. The friends eat Fotiaoqiang, or "Buddha jumps over the wall," which has shark fin and Shaoxing wine in it.

Fuzhou eats the shellfish that he catches from the sea. He likes to wash it down with some of Fujian's oolong tea. He also loves to hike the many hills that are around, and hear the different tongues that are spoken in each town.

silkworm cocoons

sugar

Guangdong

广东

rice

Song continues his travels and meets up with his friend, Guangzhou, who lives in the wealthy province of Guangdong. They first take a trip to the Leizhou Peninsula, where they see some inactive volcanoes. They then go to the Canton Fair, which is the largest Import and Export Fair in China. While there, Guangzhou brags to Song about Guangdong being one of the richest provinces in China. They next go to Zhongshan Sun Wen Memorial Park for Sun Yat-Sen, which is a popular tourist attraction memorializing the fact that Guangdong was the homeland of the founder of modern China, Sun Yat-Sen. They end their day with a meal of worldwide famous Cantonese cuisine at a restaurant overlooking the Pearl River. The Pearl River is the third largest in China, and is formed by convergence of the Xi (West), Bei (North), and Dong (East) branches.

Guangzhou passes mountains
and a few quiet volcanoes.
She thinks about her home
and the beauty that it shows.
Guangdong's a wealthy province,
and the birthplace of great men.
What comes to mind are heros,
like the leader Sun Yat-Sen.

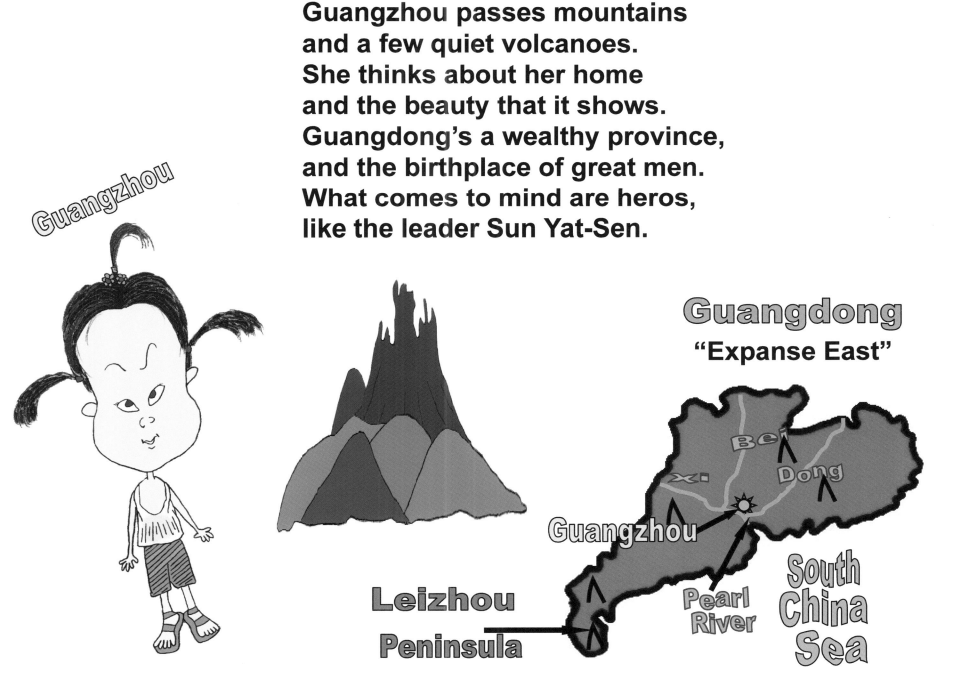

Macau

澳门

Tourism/gambling

Clothing industry

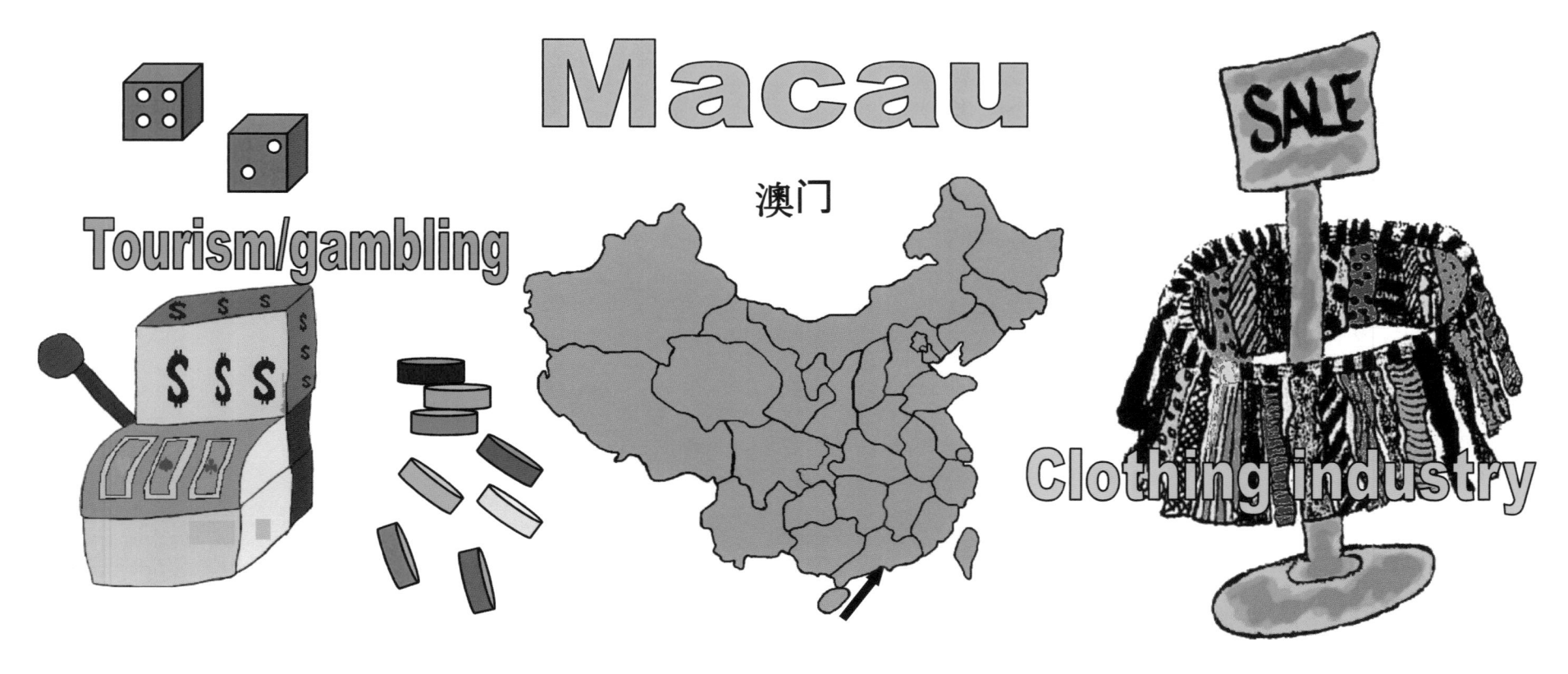

Song's next visit is to his friend, Macau, who lives in the Macau Special Administrative Region to the west of the Pearl River Delta. This is one of the richest and most densely populated cities in the entire world! Macau's mother is a tailor. He tells Song that textile and garment manufacturing help give Macau its wealth. Song and Macau hear both Cantonese and Portuguese spoken as they make their way past restaurants serving foods of the same two ethnicities. Macau tells Song that he's in luck, because he's visiting just in time to go to the Macau Grand Prix in the Macau Peninsula. They walk toward streets that have been converted to racetracks!

Macau makes his home
not far from the sea…
A rich and crowded place
that has the great Grand Prix.
For meals he has his choice;
tonight it's Cantonese.
Tomorrow he might dine instead
on food that's Portuguese.

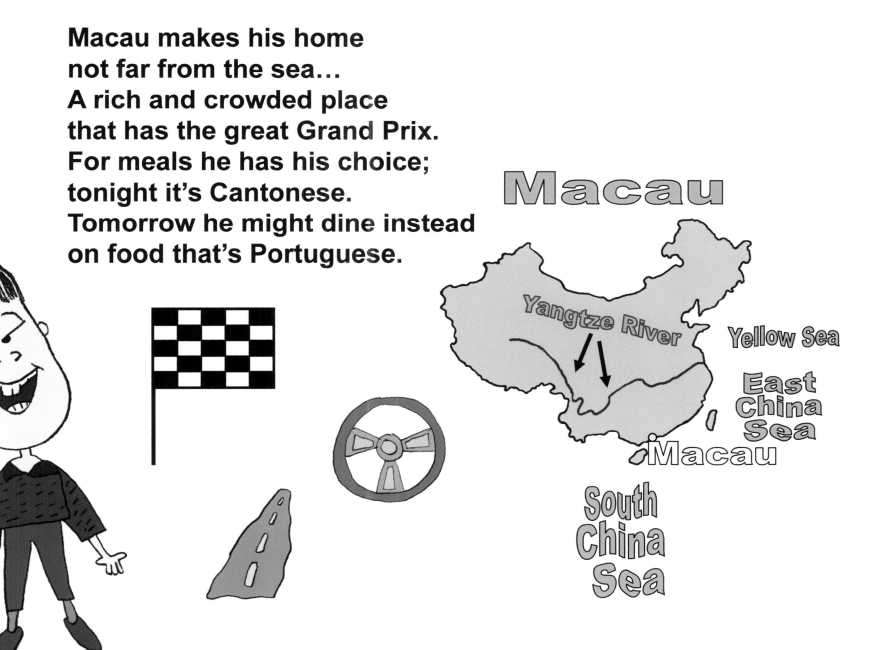

Hong Kong

香港

finance

business

Song next visits his friend Hong Kong, who lives in the mountainous Hong Kong Special Administrative Region on the Pearl River Delta. Song learns that Hong Kong, like Macau, is one of the most densely populated regions in the world, and is not considered part of mainland China. He also finds out that Hong Kong has a strongly capitalist economy, and is a major center for business, culture, and finance. The region also follows a policy known as "one country, two systems," which allows Hong Kong to be mostly self-governing. Walking around, the two boys see so many skyscrapers! Song is told that Hong Kong has the largest number of skyscrapers in the entire world! Song can tell from seeing restaurants selling traditional Chinese cuisine next to restaurants selling fast food how the description "a place where the East Meets West" applies. Hong Kong's mixing of Chinese ethnicity and English culture come from a time when Hong Kong was under British control.

Hong Kong sees his dad go out
with suit and business papers,
walking past the city lights
and many tall skyscrapers.
He eats some dim sum here,
and has some lo mein there.
Then he has some fries, a shake,
and burger medium-rare.

Hong Kong

"Fragrant
Harbour"

Yangtze River

Yellow Sea

Hong Kong

East
China
Sea

South
China
Sea

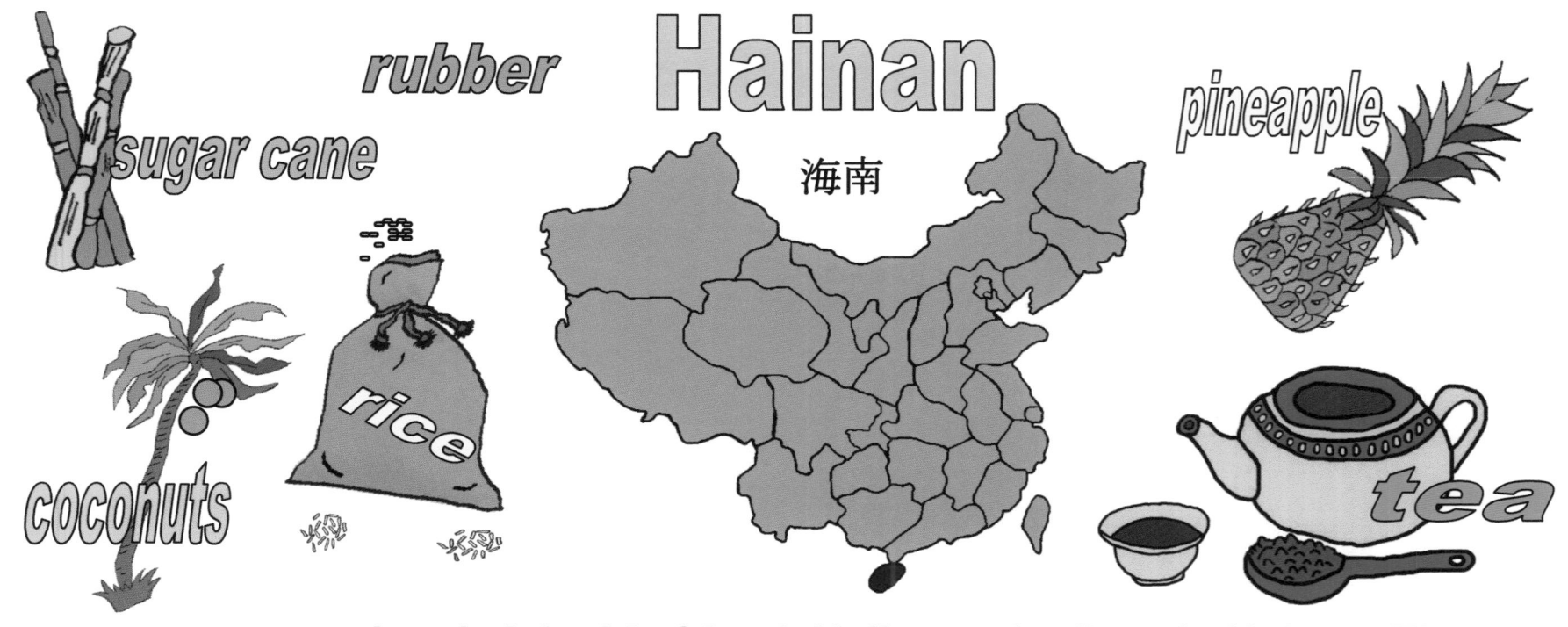

Song moves onward and visits his friend, Haikou, who lives in Hainan. The two pals take long strolls along the eastern coast of the province, with a beautiful white sand beach under their feet. They admire the lovely green water rolling onto it, and the plentiful trees around them. Haikou points out a Hainan Gibbon in the distance! It is one of the world's most endangered primates. Haikou tells Song that Hainan wasn't always the wonderful tropical paradise for tourists that it is now. China's smallest province actually used to be a place to where criminals and disgraced officials were exiled! It starts to rain, and they both duck into a restaurant to eat a dish of traditional, mildly seasoned Hainan cuisine. As they eat, pellets of rain loudly pound on the rooftop of the restaurant. Haikou tells Song that the eastern part of Hainan can get hit hard by typhoons, and there tends to be a lot of flooding as a result.

Haikou walks along a beach
while eating sugar cane.
She sees some clouds up in the sky
and knows there will be rain.
She doesn't see a place to duck…
no houses, roofs, or huts.
All she has for shelter is
a tree with coconuts.

Hainan

"South of the Sea"

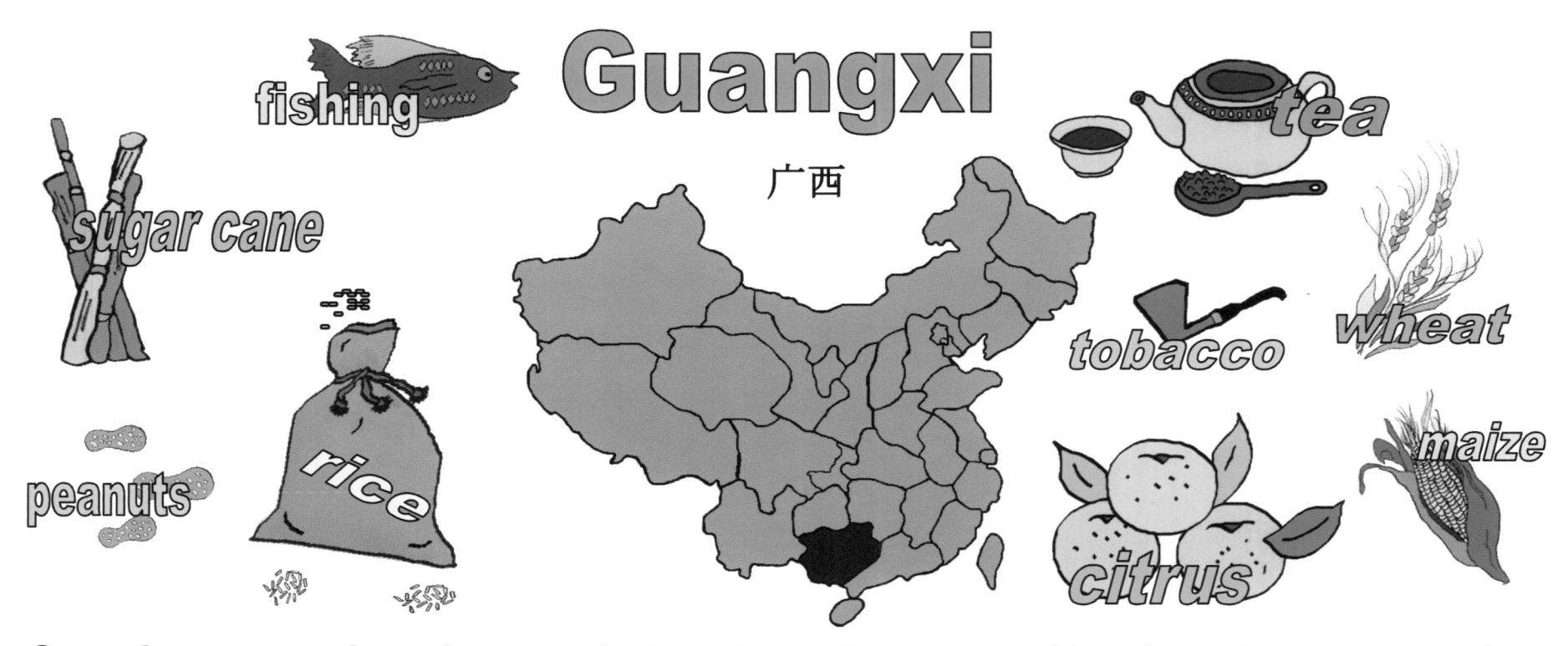

Guangxi

广西

fishing

tea

sugar cane

tobacco

wheat

maize

peanuts

rice

citrus

Song keeps moving along and stops in at the home of his friend, Nanning, who lives in the mountainous Guangxi Zhuang Special Autonomous Region in the People's Republic of China. Nanning belongs to the Zhuang ethnic group, which resides mainly in southern provinces like Guangxi and Guizhou. The friends visit the famous town of Guilin by the Lijiang River, and they marvel at its amazing karst peaks. These formations arose from sea-bed movements millions of years ago that laid down limestone deposits, which wind and water eroded into amazing shapes. Song and Nanning finish their day by dining on rice noodles in a nearby restaurant. As they eat, Nanning tells Song about the Longsheng rice terraces, which are said to be some of the steepest in the world!

Of many wondrous sights to see,
young Nanning often speaks.
Yet nothing strikes her fancy
like Guangxi's great karst peaks.
Their shapes stand out as silhouettes
against the mighty sky.
She sees them while she's standing
on a rice terrace so high.

Guizhou

贵州

Song's last stop is at the home of his friend, Guiyang, a Miao who lives in the province of Guizhou. The two friends do a little sight-seeing, and Song notices that there is a large number of covered bridges throughout the province. Guiyang explains to Song that these covered bridges, called "Wind and Rain Bridges," were built by the Dong minority people and are very common in Guizhou. Their last visit is to the Huangguoshu Waterfall, the largest waterfall in all of China!

While hiking on the Yunnan-Guizhou plateau, Song meets another buddy of his: Cai, who is coming from the direction of Yunnan province, just to the west.

 "I heard you were over in Guizhou," said Cai to Song. "I'm going to go on another journey through central China...want to come?"

Guiyang

Guiyang sees a bridge and grins.
It's covered for the rain and winds.
A waterfall so big and vast
is waiting for Guiyang to pass.

Guizhou

Yunnan-Guizhou
Plateau

Huangguoshu
Waterfall

Guiyang

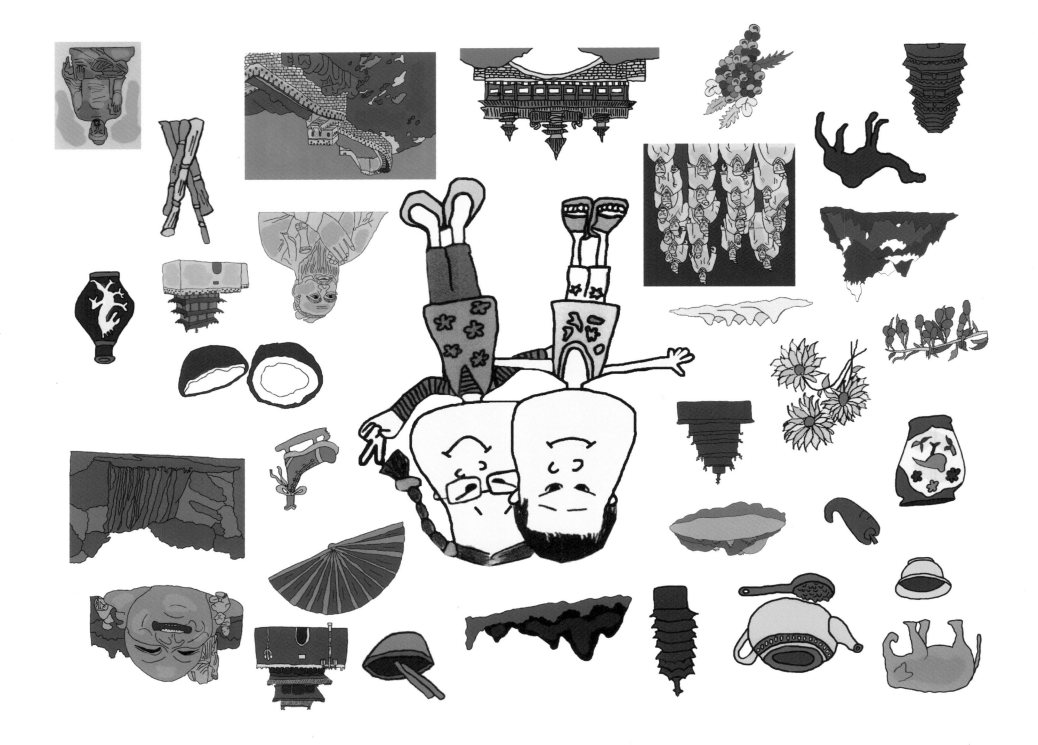

Written with love for Emily Paula, Vanessa Qu, Mae, Jian, Ellen Lei, Elizabeth Jean Fu, and Lulu Anodyne Xi

In memory of Jean Marie Casey

Dedicated to Daniel Ward Westlake, Joan Patricia Westlake, Amanda Mei Westlake, Robert John Appleyard, Mary Eileen Appleyard, Carlos Luis Hernandez, Patricia Semper Hernandez, Christopher William Casey, Denis Patrick Maroney, Jeanine Maroney, David Michael Smith, Lisa Genene Smith

Also dedicated to Shari, Joe, Marisa and Sarah Ostrowski and Jake, Connie, and Ava Guralnick

A special thank you to the following for their encouragement, support, and valuable feedback:
Irwin and Jun Weisberg, Sheila and Joseph Weisberg, Mae Gold, Larry Weisberg, Victor Gold and Aimee, Karen Sclare, Dan and Susan Acker, Estelle and Jerry Altman, David and Eva Acker, Jane Yoffe, Rachel Acker, Jonathan and Michelle Yoffe, Jingrui Jiang, Chu Chen, Kelly and Liam Gousios, Kenny Colville, Brenda Silver, Sophia Adamia, Arghya Ray, Rosemary Barrett, Suzanne Meyer, Dorna Baumann, Elizabeth Curry, Joanne Choi, Lisa Kallianidis, Karla Gregory, Julie Langbort, Barbara Segal, Judi Klevan, Diane Marotta, Deven and Elizabeth Cohen, Ann Penta, Lynette King, Julie and Scott Zimmett, Kristen Kerouac, Mary Small, Cindy Brunelle, Jennifer Metcalf, Allison Anneser, Leona Palmer, Holly Pettit, Frank G. Williams, Shirley and Frank Williams, Debra Daigle, Franny Schlickman.

Personal proceeds for the purchase of "All Across China" will support breast cancer research.

Printed in the United States

145231LV00004B